Practice Tests
for

Baron

Psychology
Fifth Edition

Prepared by
Thomas T. Jackson
Fort Hays State University

Allyn and Bacon
Boston • London • Toronto • Sydney • Tokyo • Singapore

TABLE OF CONTENTS

Introduction

INTRODUCTION

These practice tests were prepared for use with Robert A. Baron's *Psychology* (5th Edition). Each chapter has one practice test covering the material in the chapter. Each test has 25 multiple choice questions with four alternatives for each question. The questions are similar to those that may be given to you in tests for this particular course. Each practice test is followed by the same questions with justifications written for each of the four answers and page numbers associated with the questions. The answer justifications are then followed by a list of the question numbers with the answer for each question.

For your convenience in looking up justifications, page numbers, and answers, each practice test lists the chapter from which the test was taken. In addition, each question is numbered with the chapter number along with a number between 1 and 25. For example, Item 11.4 from is from Chapter 11 and is the fourth question from that chapter. There is a range of difficulty for the questions, and some of the questions are fairly challenging, so for each question, select the best answer for that question.

A suggestion for using these practice tests would be for you to study the textbook chapter and then take a practice test to see how well you grasped the material. After taking the test, look up the answers that you missed in the justifications section and write down the page numbers of any questions you missed and look up that material in the textbook and make sure that you understand the material. You might then retake the practice test and see how you scored. Again, look up any material that you are not quite sure of, using the page numbers in the justifications section.

These practice tests can help you become familiar with the material in the textbook, as well as help you become familiar with the type of questions asked over the material. Such familiarity should be of benefit to you as you progress through the course.

Good fortune to you in your psychology course.

Tom Jackson, PhD
Fort Hays State University

Chapter 1 - Practice Test

1.1   In your textbook, psychology is defined as
    a.   the science of the mind.
    b.   the science of behavior processes and mind processes.
    c.   the science of mind processes and cognitive processes.
    d.   the science of behavior and cognitive processes.

1.2   John B. Watson argued that psychology should involve the study of actions that can be observed and measured, which was the foundation of _____.
    a.   behaviorism.
    b.   functionalism.
    c.   structuralism.
    d.   humanism.

1.3   The question of "stability versus change" involves the extent to which
    a.   psychology's experimental findings remain stable or change over time.
    b.   characteristics and behavior of individuals remain stable or change over time.
    c.   behavior in experiments remains stable over a long period of time or change over this period.
    d.   IQ measures stay the same or change over time.

1.4   Ralph drives a drag racer on the weekends and is always very excited every time he finishes his runs down the strip. The _____ would explain his behavior by pointing out humans' inherited desire for excitement.
    a.   cognitive perspective.
    b.   behavioral perspective.
    c.   psychodynamic perspective.
    d.   biological perspective.

1.5   The greatest number of psychologists are in the subfields of
    a.   clinical and counseling psychology.
    b.   developmental and educational psychology.
    c.   cognitive and industrial psychology.
    d.   social and organizational psychology.

1.6   The branch of psychology that suggests that humans possess a large number of psychological mechanisms that help us deal with issues related to survival is called
    a.   structuralist psychology.
    b.   functionalist psychology.
    c.   evolutionary psychology.
    d.   behaviorist psychology.

1.7   The four essential components of the scientific method are
    a.   intuition, objectivity, accuracy, open-mindedness.
    b.   accuracy, creativity, internal validity, objectivity.
    c.   objectivity, training, skepticism, external validity.
    d.   accuracy, objectivity, skepticism, open-mindedness.

1.8   The tendency to perceive that just because something is easy to remember it must be important represents
     a.   the confirmation bias.
     b.   the representative heuristic.
     c.   the availability heuristic.
     d.   the holistic bias.

1.9   Being skeptical, keeping an open mind, and not jumping to conclusions are characteristics of
     a.   a negative approach to life.
     b.   dispositional attribute.
     c.   critical thinking.
     d.   analytical thinking.

1.10   In the survey method, trying to get a large enough group of people that is representative of the larger population is a problem of
     a.   correlation.
     b.   definition.
     c.   accessibility.
     d.   sampling.

1.11   If the number of storks (birds) in an area is fairly high, the number of human births 9 months later will be fairly high. Therefore, storks cause babies. This example points out the difficulty with
     a.   experimentation.
     b.   case method.
     c.   correlation.
     d   ornithology.

1.12   Relationship is to cause-and-effect as
     a.   case study is to naturalistic observation.
     b.   naturalistic observation is to case study.
     c.   correlation is to experiment.
     d.   experiment is to correlation.

1.13   Lisa is getting ready to conduct an experiment and, for convenience, has decided to put all students from an 8:30am class in the experimental group and all students from the 2:30pm class in the control group. Lisa has just violated the condition of
     a.   random assignment of participants.
     b.   equality of variables.
     c.   cause-and-effect.
     d.   replication of comparable conditions.

1.14   Which of the following is an important reason for using animals as research subjects in psychology?
     a.   There are no ethical rules that limit what research can be performed with animals.
     b.   All important human psychological abilities can be found in animals.
     c.   Some kinds of research are allowed with animals but not with humans.
     d.   Nothing: there are no important, ethically justified reasons for using animals in research.

1.15   The reason that you should begin studying with an overview of the material to be studied is that memory research indicates that it is easier to retain information if it is placed in a(n)
     a.   ordered list.
     b.   cognitive framework.
     c.   conative association.
     d.   rehearsal format.

1.16   The view that knowledge can be gained through logic and careful reasoning is
        a. rationalism.
        b. empiricism.
        c. functionalism.
        d. behaviorism.

1.17   One of the major contributions of functionalism was the emphasis on
        a. structure of consciousness.
        b. theoretical implications of consciousness.
        c. behavioral aspects of consciousness.
        d. practical aspects of consciousness.

1.18   The study of _____ is one of the most vigorous areas of research in psychology.
        a. affective processes
        b. behavioral processes
        c. cognitive processes
        d. conative processes

1.19   Trying to determine the extent to which behavior is influenced by logic or by emotion involves the
        question of
        a. stability versus change.
        b. rationality versus irrationality.
        c. nature versus nurture.
        d. determinism versus free will.

1.20   Psychologists who study aspects of basic psychological processes such as perception, learning, and
        motivation are called _____ psychologists.
        a. social
        b. cognitive
        c. phenomenological
        d. experimental

1.21   An applied psychologist is one who
        a. prescribes and monitors the effects of medications.
        b. does research and uses it to solve practical problems.
        c. conducts research that is purely theoretical and abstract.
        d. explores the subconscious through dream analysis.

1.22   The main purpose of theories is to
        a. explain.
        b. postdict.
        c. evaluate.
        d. summarize.

1.23   Lisa is considered a critical thinker, therefore she would have which of the following characteristics?
        a. jumps to conclusions
        b. keeps an open mind
        c. is easily persuaded
        d. has a negative slant on things

1.24   If one wants to know the cause of behavior, one should use
     a.   observation.
     b.   correlation.
     c.   experimentation.
     d.   surveys.

1.25   Unintended effects caused by researchers on participants's behavior are called
     a.   deception effects.
     b.   participant effects.
     c.   experimenter effects.
     d.   confound effects.

Chapter 1 - Practice Test Answer Justifications

1.1 In your textbook, psychology is defined as
   a. The science of mind is incorrect because the concept of mind is too ambiguous. Review page 5 in your textbook.
   b. Mind processes is incorrect because of the ambiguity of the concept of mind. Review page 5 in your textbook.
   c. This answer is incorrect because it does not include some reference to behavior. Review page 5 in your textbook.
   d. For more information, see page 5 in your textbook.

1.2 John B. Watson argued that psychology should involve the study of actions that can be observed and measured, which was the foundation of _____.
   a. For more information, see page 7 in your textbook.
   b. Functionalism is incorrect because it emphasized the function of consciousness. Review page 7 in your textbook.
   c. Structuralism is incorrect because it emphasized the elements of consciousness. Review page 7 in your textbook.
   d. Humanism is incorrect because it emphasized the role of the future, not the past. Review page 7 in your textbook.

1.3 The question of "stability versus change" involves the extent to which
   a. Psychology's experimental findings are incorrect because they depend upon the participants, upon the instruments, the social conditions, etc. Review page 10 in your textbook.
   b. For more information, see page 10 in your textbook.
   c. Behavior in experiments is incorrect because it is too specific, and not one of the grand questions of psychology. Review page 10 in your textbook.
   d. IQ measures is incorrect because it is too specific and not one of the grand questions of psychology. Review page 10 in your textbook.

1.4 Ralph drives a drag racer on the weekends and is always very excited every time he finishes his runs down the strip. The _____ would explain his behavior by pointing out humans' inherited desire for excitement.
   a. The cognitive perspective is incorrect because the emphasis is on the inherited, not cognitive, aspects of excitement. Review page 11 in your textbook.
   b. The behavioral perspective is incorrect because the emphasis is on the inherited, not behavioral, aspects of excitement. Review page 11 in your textbook.
   c. The psychodynamic perspective is incorrect because the emphasis is on inherited, not unconscious, aspects of excitement. Review page 11 in your textbook.
   d. For more information, see page 11 in your textbook.

1.5 The greatest number of psychologists are in the subfields of
   a. For more information, see page 13 in your textbook.
   b. This answer is incorrect because only about 11% of all psychologists are in these subfields. Review page 13 in your textbook.
   c. This answer is incorrect because only about 18% of all psychologists are in these subfields. Review page 13 in your textbook.
   d. This answer is incorrect because only about 10% of all psychologists are in these subfields. Review page 13 in your textbook.

1.6   The branch of psychology that suggests that humans possess a large number of psychological mechanisms that help us deal with issues related to survival is called
- a. Structuralist psychology is incorrect because it deals with the elements of consciousness. Review page 15 in your textbook.
- b. Functionalist psychology is incorrect because it deals with the function of consciousness. Review page 15 in your textbook.
- c. For more information, see page 15 in your textbook.
- d. Behaviorist psychology is incorrect because it deals with the observable behavior of an individual. Review page 15 in your textbook.

1.7   The four essential components of the scientific method are
- a. This answer is incorrect because of the inclusion of intuition. Review page 20 in your textbook.
- b. This answer is incorrect because of the inclusion of creativity and internal validity. Review page 20 in your textbook.
- c. This answer is incorrect because of the inclusion of training and external validity. Review page 20 in your textbook.
- d. For more information, see page 20 in your textbook.

1.8   The tendency to perceive that just because something is easy to remember it must be important represents
- a. Confirmation bias is incorrect because it addresses the impact of information that supports our already held views. Review page 22 in your textbook.
- b. Representative heuristic is incorrect because it addresses the influence of how common a recalled event might be in a class of events. Review page 22 in your textbook.
- c. For more information, see page 22 in your textbook.
- d. Holistic bias is incorrect because it addresses nothing concerning how easy something is to remember. Review page 22 in your textbook.

1.9   Being skeptical, keeping an open mind, and not jumping to conclusions are characteristics of
- a. This answer is incorrect because none of these characteristics are specifically negative. Review page 23 in your textbook.
- b. Dispositional attribute is incorrect because it concerns the internal attributions someone makes about the causes of behavior. Review page 23 in your textbook.
- c. For more information, see page 23 in your textbook.
- d. This answer is incorrect because an individual can analyze something without using all of the characteristics listed. Review page 23 in your textbook.

1.10   In the survey method, trying to get a large enough group of people that is representative of the larger population is a problem of
- a. Correlation is incorrect because it deals with relationships, not representativeness. Review page 25 in your textbook.
- b. definition is incorrect because it is not necessarily related to representativeness. Review page 25 in your textbook.
- c. Accessibility is incorrect because accessibility is not necessarily related to representativeness. Review page 25 in your textbook.
- d. For more information, see page 25 in your textbook.

1.11   If the number of storks (birds) in an area is fairly high, the number of human births 9 months later will be fairly high. Therefore, storks cause babies. This example points out the difficulty with
- a. Experimentation is incorrect because there is no manipulation of variables, only measurement. Review page 27 in your textbook.
- b. This answer is incorrect because the case method would not address the number of animals in a specific area. Review page 27 in your textbook.
- c. For more information, see page 27 in your textbook.
- d. Ornithology is incorrect because it deals with birds, not cause and effect relationships among birds and humans. Review page 27 in your textbook.

1.12   Relationship is to cause-and-effect as
   a.   This answer is incorrect because both of these methods involve relationship. Review page 28 in your textbook.
   b.   This answer is incorrect because both of these methods involve relationship. Review page 28 in your textbook.
   c.   For more information, see page 28 in your textbook.
   d.   This answer is incorrect because experiment involves cause-and-effect while correlation involves relationship. Review page 28 in your textbook.

1.13   Lisa is getting ready to conduct an experiment and, for convenience, has decided to put all students from an 8:30am class in the experimental group and all students from the 2:30pm class in the control group. Lisa has just violated the condition of
   a.   For more information, see page 30 in your textbook.
   b.   This answer is incorrect because experimentation does not require equality of variables. Review page 30 in your textbook.
   c.   This answer is incorrect because there is no such condition in an experiment. Review page 30 in your textbook.
   d.   This answer is incorrect because such replication occurs in order to compare conditions in two or more experiments. Review page 30 in your textbook.

1.14   Which of the following is an important reason for using animals as research subjects in psychology?
   a.   This answer is incorrect because there are definite ethical rules that apply to research with animals. Review page 34 in your textbook.
   b.   This answer is incorrect because not all human psychological abilities are found in humans. Review page 34 in your textbook.
   c.   For more information, see page 34 in your textbook.
   d.   This answer is incorrect because there are no absolute answers in this area - each researcher must decide. Review page 34 in your textbook.

1.15   The reason that you should begin studying with an overview of the material to be studied is that memory research indicates that it is easier to retain information if it is placed in a:
   a.   This answer is incorrect because a list may be important but it does not give you a "big picture" view of the material with associations. Review page 36 in your textbook.
   b.   For more information, see page 36 in your textbook.
   c.   This answer is incorrect because the emotion associated with material is not necessarily related to an overview. Review page 36 in your textbook.
   d.   This answer is incorrect because, while rehearsal is important, it is not related to the overview of the material. Review page 36 in your textbook.

1.16   The view that knowledge can be gained through logic and careful reasoning is
   a.   For more information, see page 6 in your textbook.
   b.   This answer is incorrect because empiricism is associated with observation and numbers. Review page 6 in your textbook.
   c.   This answer is incorrect because functionalism involves the use of experiments. Review page 6 in your textbook.
   d.   This answer is incorrect because behaviorism involves observation and experimentation. Review page 6 in your textbook.

1.17   One of the major contributions of functionalism was the emphasis on
    a.   This answer is incorrect because functionalism was interested in the function of consciousness. Review page 7 in your textbook.
    b.   This answer is incorrect because functionalism was interested in the practical aspects of consciousness. Review page 7 in your textbook.
    c.   This answer is incorrect because functionalism emphasized the function of consciousness. Review page 7 in your textbook.
    d.   For more information, see page 7 in your textbook.

1.18   The study of _____ is one of the most vigorous areas of research in psychology.
    a.   This answer is incorrect because research emphases have moved away from the study of affective processes exclusively. Review page 9 in your textbook.
    b.   This answer is incorrect because research emphases have moved away from the study of behavioral processes exclusively. Review page 9 in your textbook.
    c.   For more information, see page 9 in your textbook.
    d.   This answer is incorrect because conative processes are essentially behavior processes, which research emphases have moved away exclusively. Review page 9 in your textbook.

1.19   Trying to determine the extent to which behavior is influenced by logic or by emotion involves the question of
    a.   This answer is incorrect because stability versus change involves the developmental processes of the various systems of an organism. Review page 10 in your textbook.
    b.   For more information, see page 10 in your textbook.
    c.   This answer is incorrect because nature versus nurture involves the contribution of each of these elements to the development of an organism. Review page 10 in your textbook.
    d.   This answer is incorrect because determinism versus free will involves the philosophical positions of whether behavior is affected primarily by the past or the future. Review page 10 in your textbook.

1.20   Psychologists who study aspects of basic psychological processes such as perception, learning, and motivation are called _____ psychologists.
    a.   This answer is incorrect because social psychologists study behavior in social settings. Review page 13 in your textbook.
    b.   This answer is incorrect because cognitive psychologists study how cognitive processes affect behavior in various realms. Review page 13 in your textbook.
    c.   This answer is incorrect because phenomenological psychologists study behavior as it occurs, not with experiments. Review page 13 in your textbook.
    d.   For more information, see page 13 in your textbook.

1.21   An applied psychologist is one who
    a.   This answer is incorrect because such an individual would be a physician. Review page 17 in your textbook.
    b.   For more information, see page 17 in your textbook.
    c.   This answer is incorrect because such an individual would be conducting research that might or might not be applied. Review page 17 in your textbook.
    d.   This answer is incorrect because such an individual would be a psychotherapist. Review page 17 in your textbook.

1.22   The main purpose of theories is to
    a.   For more information, see page 20 in your textbook.
    b.   This answer is incorrect because prediction, not postdiction, is a concern of theories. Review page 20 in your textbook.
    c.   This answer is incorrect because evaluation involves value judgments on the part of someone. Review page 20 in your textbook.
    d.   This answer is incorrect because summarization would be after data had been collected and would be a mechanical process. Review page 20 in your textbook.

1.23   Lisa is considered a critical thinker, therefore she would have which of the following characteristics?
   a.   This answer is incorrect because jumping to conclusions would not involve evaluative thinking. Review page 23 in your textbook.
   b.   For more information, see page 23 in your textbook.
   c.   This answer is incorrect because a critical thinker would evaluate all aspects of an argument before being persuaded, and would not be easily persuaded. Review page 23 in your textbook.
   d.   This answer is incorrect because a critical thinker would have a neutral view until material had been presented. Review page 23 in your textbook.

1.24   If one wants to know the cause of behavior, one should use
   a.   This answer is incorrect because observation will not provide objective reasons for a behavior. Review page 29 in your textbook.
   b.   This answer is incorrect because correlation provides information about relationships, not cause and effect. Review page 29 in your textbook.
   c.   For more information, see page 29 in your textbook.
   d.   This answer is incorrect because surveys are tools to gather information, not a method of determining cause. Review page 29 in your textbook.

1.25   Unintended effects caused by researchers on participants's behavior are called
   a.   This answer is incorrect because deception effects would be intended. Review page 31 in your textbook.
   b.   This answer is incorrect because participant effects would be the result of the participants, not the researchers. Review page 31 in your textbook.
   c.   For more information, see page 31 in your textbook.
   d.   This answer is incorrect because confound effects are due to unintended combinations of variables that are not controlled. Review page 31 in your textbook.

Chapter 1 - Practice Test Answers

Question	Answer
1.1	d
1.2	a
1.3	b
1.4	d
1.5	a
1.6	c
1.7	d
1.8	c
1.9	c
1.10	d
1.11	c
1.12	c
1.13	a
1.14	c
1.15	b
1.16	a
1.17	d
1.18	c
1.19	b
1.20	d
1.21	b
1.22	a
1.23	b
1.24	c
1.25	c

Chapter 2 - Practice Test

2.1   The three basic parts of the neuron are
   a.   vesicles, gray matter, and the synapse.
   b.   glial cells, nodes of Ranvier, and synaptic terminals.
   c.   cell body, axon, and dendrites.
   d.   myelin sheath, cell body, and dendrites.

2.2   The speed of conduction on an axon is fastest if the axon is
   a.   myelinated.
   b.   hyperpolarized.
   c.   sensitized.
   d.   lacking nodes of Ranvier.

2.3   What will happen if the level of excitation inside a neuron goes higher than the cell's threshold?
   a.   It will become polarized.
   b.   It will break down and stop functioning.
   c.   It will trigger an action potential.
   d.   It will produce extra myelin.

2.4   Communications between neurons is initiated by
   a.   ion exchange across the synapse.
   b.   neurotransmitters being released in the synapse.
   c.   action potentials along the dendrites.
   d.   release of negative ions.

2.5   The neurotransmitter that is released at most junctions between motor neurons and muscle cells is
   a.   GABA.
   b.   serotonin.
   c.   norepinephrine.
   d.   acetylcholine.

2.6   The major divisions of the nervous system are the
   a.   somatic and autonomic.
   b.   central and subcentral.
   c.   central and peripheral.
   d.   brain and somatic.

2.7   _____ nerves carry information to the brain, while _____ nerves carry information away from the brain.
   a.   Efferent; afferent
   b.   Afferent; efferent
   c.   Monosynaptic; polysynaptic
   d.   Polysynaptic; monosynaptic

2.8   The part of the autonomic nervous system that conserves the body's energy is known as the
   a.   somatic nervous system.
   b.   sympathetic nervous system.
   c.   peripheral nervous system.
   d.   parasympathetic nervous system.

12

2.9 The _____ is the brain structure that plays a very important role in the regulation of the autonomic nervous system and a role in eating and drinking.
a. thalamus
b. pons
c. pituitary gland
d. hypothalamus.

2.10 The occipital lobe is a part of the cerebral cortex and is involved in
a. vision.
b. hearing.
c. touch.
d. speech.

2.11 Research indicates that for most people, the function of speech is located in the
a. right cerebral hemisphere.
b. occipital lobe.
c. left cerebral hemisphere.
d. frontal lobe.

2.12 When Lisa was making a decision about her college major, a PET scan of her brain showed high activity in her
a. left cerebral hemisphere.
b. right cerebral hemisphere.
c. hypothalamus.
d. thalamus.

2.13 The brain imaging method that involves measuring the differences in the brain's magnetic field based upon the electric current produced when neurons fire is called
a. CT.
b. SQUID.
c. MRI.
d. PET .

2.14 It appears that our brains process information in a
a. serial fashion.
b. parallel fashion.
c. contiguous fashion.
d. successive fashion.

2.15 If identical twins who were separated at birth and raised in different environments show marked similarities in behavior, it is probably because
a. their adoptive parents are very similar to their birth parents.
b. their behavior is being affected by their biological, genetic inheritance.
d. twins have a subconscious telepathic link that makes them similar.
d. all children are very similar, no matter how they are raised or by whom.

2.16 Which of the following carries information away from the cell body of a nerve cell?
a. dendrite
b. astrocyte
c. glial cells
d. axon

2.17 The action potential is a(n)
a. chemical used to transmit nerve messages.
b. all-or-none electrical potential change inside a nerve.
c. level of activation each cell tries to maintain.
d. type of nerve cell that carries muscle commands.

2.18 Endorphins are chemicals in the brain that produce effects similar to
a. caffeine.
b. marijuana.
c. LSD.
d. morphine.

2.19 Structures that secrete hormones directly into the bloodstream are called
a. basal ganglia.
b. endocrine glands.
c. limbic glands.
d. secretion glands.

2.20 The structure called the "great relay station" that receives input from all senses except olfaction is the
a. cortex.
b. hypothalamus.
c. cerebellum.
d. thalamus.

2.21 The outer surface of the two hemispheres of the brain is called the
a. corpus callosum.
b. medulla.
c. pons.
d. cortex.

2.22 The brain's ability to retrain an area to compensate for damage to another area refers to
a. differentiation.
b. specialization.
c. contralateralization.
d. plasticity.

2.23 The process of _____ involves damaging part of an animal's brain by implanting electrodes in specific areas of interest.
a. magnetic resonance imaging
b. exorcism
c. ablation
e. positron emission tomography

2.24 Twin studies are useful in disentangling the relative roles of _____ in a given form of behavior.
a. cognitive and emotional factors
b. genetic and environmental factors
c. social and individual factors
d. cognitive and conative factors

2.25 The finding that men, compared to women, score higher in dominance motivation provides support for the
_____.
a. biological perspective
b. evolutionary perspective
c. social-cultural perspective
d. behavioral perspective

Chapter 2 - Practice Test Answer Justifications

2.1   The three basic parts of the neuron are
   a.   This answer is incorrect because none of the items listed are basic parts of the neuron. Vesicles and synapse are related to the function of the neuron, and gray matter is related to the structure of the brain. Review page44 in your textbook.
   b.   This answer is incorrect because glial cells and the nodes of Ranvier are related to the myelin sheath of the axon, and synaptic terminals are related to the connection of one neuron to another. Review page 44 in your textbook.
   c.   For more information, see page 44 in your textbook.
   d.   This answer is incorrect because the myelin sheath is related to an axon specifically. Review page 44 in your textbook.

2.2   What will happen if the level of excitation inside a neuron goes higher than the cell's threshold?
   a.   This answer is incorrect because the neuron becomes depolarized at this point. Review page 46 in your textbook.
   b.   This answer is incorrect because the neuron continues to function but in a different manner. Review page 46 in your textbook.
   c.   For more information, see page 46 in your textbook.
   d.   This answer is incorrect because glial cells produce myelin. Review page 46 in your textbook.

2.3   The speed of conduction on an axon is fastest if the axon is
   a.   For more information, see page 46 in your textbook.
   b.   Hyperpolarized is incorrect because it is not related to speed of conduction of an axon. Review page 46 in your textbook.
   c.   Sensitized is incorrect because it is not related to the speed of conduction of an axon. Review page 46 in your textbook.
   d.   This answer is incorrect because the lack of nodes of Ranvier would indicate the axon was not myelinated and would therefore conduct at a slower speed. Review page 46 in your textbook.

2.4   Communications between neurons is initiated by
   a.   This answer is incorrect because ions are exchanged within, not between neurons. Review page 48 in your textbook.
   b.   For more information, see page 48 in your textbook.
   c.   This answer is incorrect because action potentials occur in the cell body. Review page 48 in your textbook.
   d.   This answer is incorrect because ions are exchanged within, not between neurons. Review page 48 in your textbook.

2.5   The neurotransmitter that is released at most junctions between motor neurons and muscle cells is
   a.   GABA is incorrect because it is primarily related to inhibition in the brain, not muscle action. Review page 48 in your textbook.
   b.   Serotonin is incorrect because it is primarily related to mood and arousal, not muscle action. Review page 48 in your textbook.
   c.   Norepinephrine is incorrect because it is primarily related to alertness and wakefulness, not muscle action. Review page 48 in your textbook.
   d.   For more information, see page 48 in your textbook.

2.6   The major divisions of the nervous system are the
   a.   This answer is incorrect because these two systems are subdivisions of the peripheral nervous system. Review page 50 in your textbook.
   b.   This answer is incorrect because subcentral is not a specific division of the nervous system. Review page 50 in your textbook.
   c.   For more information, see page 50 in your textbook.
   d.   This answer is incorrect because the brain is part of the central nervous system and somatic is a subdivision of the peripheral nervous system. Review page 50 in your textbook.

2.7 _____ nerves carry information to the brain, while _____ nerves carry information away from the brain.
   a. This answer is incorrect because efferent nerves carry information away from the brain and afferent carry information to the brain. Review page 50 in your textbook.
   b. For more information, see page 50 in your textbook.
   c. This answer is incorrect because these terms indicate the synaptic potential for a neuron. Review page 50 in your textbook.
   d. This answer is incorrect because these terms indicate the synaptic potential for a neuron. Review page 50 in your textbook.

2.8 The part of the autonomic nervous system that conserves the body's energy is known as the
   a. This answer is incorrect because the somatic nervous system is a subdivision of the peripheral nervous system. Review page 52 in your textbook.
   b. This answer is incorrect because the sympathetic nervous system is related to expenditure of energy. Review page 52 in your textbook.
   c. This answer is incorrect because the peripheral nervous system is a major division of the nervous system of the body. Review page 52 in your textbook.
   d. For more information, see page 52 in your textbook.

2.9 The _____ is the brain structure that plays a very important role in the regulation of the autonomic nervous system and a role in eating and drinking.
   a. The thalamus is incorrect because it is a relay station in the brain and related to all senses except smell. Review page 56 in your textbook.
   b. The pons is incorrect because it is related to all major sensory and motor activities and to basic arousal. Review page 56 in your textbook.
   c. The pituitary gland is incorrect because it is a gland and part of the endocrine system. Review page 56 in your textbook.
   d. For more information, see page 56 in your textbook.

2.10 The occipital lobe is a part of the cerebral cortex and is involved in
   a. For more information, see page 60 in your textbook.
   b. This answer is incorrect because the occipital lobe is primarily involved in vision. Review page 60 in your textbook.
   c. This answer is incorrect because the occipital lobe is primarily involved in vision. Review page 60 in your textbook.
   d. This answer is incorrect because the occipital lobe is primarily involved in vision. Review page 60 in your textbook.

2.11 Research indicates that for most people, the function of speech is located in the
   a. The right cerebral hemisphere is incorrect because it is primarily involved in motor movements, synthesis, and emotion. Review page 61 in your textbook.
   b. The occipital lobe is incorrect because it is primarily involved in vision. Review page 61 in your textbook.
   c. For more information, see page 61 in your textbook.
   d. The frontal lobe is incorrect because it is primarily involved in bodily movement. Review page 61 in your textbook.

2.12 When Lisa was making a decision about her college major, a PET scan of her brain showed high activity in her
   a. For more information, see page 63 in your textbook.
   b. This answer is incorrect because increased activity was indicated in this hemisphere after a decision had been made. Review page 63 in your textbook.
   c. This answer is incorrect because the hypothalamus is not involved in decision making. Review page 63 in your textbook.
   d. This answer is incorrect because the thalamus is not involved in decision making. Review page 63 in your textbook.

2.13   The brain imaging method that involves measuring the differences in the brain's magnetic field based upon the electric current produced when neurons fire is called
   a.   This answer is incorrect because this procedure uses X-rays to develop a two-dimensional picture of the brain. Review page 65 in your textbook.
   b.   For more information, see page 65 in your textbook.
   c.   This answer is incorrect because this procedure uses the measurement of energy waves derived from hydrogen atoms exposed to a magnetic field to provide images of the brain. Review page 65 in your textbook.
   d.   This answer is incorrect because this procedure measures blood flow in the brain to provide a map of activity in the brain. Review page 65 in your textbook.

2.14   It appears that our brains process information in a
   a.   This answer is incorrect because our brains do not process information one step at a time. Review page 67 in your textbook.
   b.   For more information, see page 67 in your textbook.
   c.   This answer is incorrect because information does not have to be connected in time and/or space to be processed by the brain. Review page 67 in your textbook.
   d.   This answer is incorrect because our brains do not process information one step at a time. Review page 67 in your textbook.

2.15   If identical twins who were separated at birth and raised in different environments show marked similarities in behavior, it is probably because
   a.   This answer is incorrect because the probability of such similarity is relatively low. Review page 75 in your textbook.
   b.   For more information, see page 75 in your textbook.
   c.   This answer is incorrect because such a link has not been found in twins. Review page 75 in your textbook.
   d.   This answer is incorrect because the diversity of humans would indicate a lack of similarity. Review page 75 in your textbook.

2.16   Which of the following carries information away from the cell body of a nerve cell?
   a.   This answer is incorrect because dendrites carry information toward the cell. Review page 44 in your textbook.
   b.   This answer is incorrect because an astrocyte is not involved in nerve cell transmission. Review page 44 in your textbook.
   c.   This answer is incorrect because glial cells are building blocks by themselves and not involved in nerve cell transmission, except for production of myelin around the axon. Review page 44 in your textbook.
   d.   For more information, see page 44 in your textbook.

2.17   The action potential is a(n)
   a.   This answer is incorrect because electrical potential not chemicals are used to transmit messages within neurons. Review page 46 in your textbook.
   b.   For more information, see page 46 in your textbook.
   c.   This answer is incorrect because the level of activation each cell tries to maintain is a resting potential. Review page 46 in your textbook.
   d.   This answer is incorrect because an action potential affects neuron transmission. Review page 46 in your textbook.

2.18   Endorphins are chemicals in the brain that produce effects similar to
   a.   This answer is incorrect because caffeine does not exhibit this effect. Review page 49 in your textbook.
   b.   This answer is incorrect because marijuana produces different effects. Review page 49 in your textbook.
   c.   This answer is incorrect because LSD has more extreme and less predictable effects. Review page 49 in your textbook.
   d.   For more information, see page 49 in your textbook.

2.19   Structures that secrete hormones directly into the bloodstream are called
   a.   This answer is incorrect because basal ganglia do not secrete hormones. Review page 52 in your textbook.
   b.   For more information, see page 52 in your textbook.
   c.   This answer is incorrect because limbic glands do not secrete hormones. Review page 52 in your textbook.
   d.   This answer is incorrect because secretion glands are not present. Review page 52 in your textbook.

2.20   The structure called the "great relay station" that receives input from all senses
       except olfaction is the
   a.   This answer is incorrect because the cortex does not receive input from all senses. Review page 57 in your textbook.
   b.   This answer is incorrect because hypothalamus receives input from a limited number of senses. Review page 57 in your textbook.
   c.   This answer is incorrect because cerebellum is primarily involved in motor activities. Review page 57 in your textbook.
   d.   For more information, see page 57 in your textbook.

2.21   The outer surface of the two hemispheres of the brain is called the
   a.   This answer is incorrect because the corpus callosum connects the two hemispheres. Review page 59 in your textbook.
   b.   This answer is incorrect because the medulla is located at the top of the brain stem. Review page 59 in your textbook.
   c.   This answer is incorrect because the pons is located at the top of the brain stem. Review page 59 in your textbook.
   d.   For more information, see page 59 in your textbook.

2.22   The brain's ability to retrain an area to compensate for damage to another area refers to
   a.   This answer is incorrect because differentiation involves differences among structures. Review page 59 in your textbook.
   b.   This answer is incorrect because specialization would involve limitations on activities. Review page 59 in your textbook.
   c.   This answer is incorrect because contralateralization would mean in contrast to lateralization which would involve less flexibility. Review page 59 in your textbook.
   d.   For more information, see page 59 in your textbook.

2.23   The process of _____ involves damaging part of an animal's brain by implanting electrodes in specific areas of interest.
   a.   This answer is incorrect because magnetic resonance imaging does not damage the brain. Review page 65 in your textbook.
   b.   This answer is incorrect because exorcism does not involve damage to the brain. Review page 65 in your textbook.
   c.   For more information, see page 65 in your textbook.
   e.   This answer is incorrect because positron emission tomography does not damage the brain. Review page 65 in your textbook.

2.24   Twin studies are useful in disentangling the relative roles of _____ in a given form of behavior.
    a.   This answer is incorrect because cognitive and emotional factors can be separated without the use of twins. Review page 74 in your textbook.
    b.   For more information, see page 74 in your textbook.
    c.   This answer is incorrect because social and individual factors can be determined without the use of twins. Review page 74 in your textbook.
    d.   This answer is incorrect because cognitive and conative factors can be determined without the use of twins. Review page 74 in your textbook.

2.25   The finding that men, compared to women, score higher in dominance motivation provides support for the _____.
    a.   This answer is incorrect because the biological perspective would not necessarily involve dominance. Review page 76 in your textbook.
    b.   For more information, see page 76 in your textbook.
    c.   This answer is incorrect because the social-cultural perspective does not provide an adequate explanation for this finding. Review page 76 in your textbook.
    d.   This answer is incorrect because the behavioral perspective is somewhat limited and does not provide and adequate explanation for this finding. Review page 76 in your textbook.

Chapter 2 - Practice Test Answers

Question	Answer
2.1	c
2.2	c
2.3	a
2.4	b
2.5	d
2.6	c
2.7	b
2.8	d
2.9	d
2.10	a
2.11	c
2.12	a
2.13	b
2.14	b
2.15	b
2.16	d
2.17	b
2.18	d
2.19	b
2.20	d
2.21	d
2.22	d
2.23	c
2.24	b
2.25	b

Chapter 3 - Practice Test

3.1   Detection is to interpretation as
    a.   difference threshold is to assigned threshold.
    b.   assigned threshold is to difference threshold.
    c.   sensation is to perception.
    d.   perception is to sensation.

3.2   The smallest magnitude of a stimulus that can be reliably discriminated from no
    stimulus at all 50% of the time is called
    a.   absolute threshold.
    b.   extrasensory threshold.
    c.   difference threshold.
    d.   petite threshold.

3.3   An experimenter has you compare the temperature of water in two different
    containers. She asks you if they feel the same or different. She is probably
    trying to determine your
    a.   subliminal threshold.
    b.   absolute threshold.
    c.   difference threshold.
    d.   frequency threshold.

3.4   The rods in the retina are photoreceptors used primarily for
    a.   distinguishing different colors in daylight.
    b.   focusing the image accurately on the retina.
    c.   night vision under conditions of dim lighting.
    d.   fine discriminations in the center of the eye.

3.5   The saccadic movements of good readers tend to be
    a.   jerky, with few backward movements.
    b.   smooth, with forward and backward movements.
    c.   jerky, with forward and backward movements.
    d.   smooth, with few backward movements.

3.6   Negative afterimages are more effectively explained by
    a.   trichromatic theory.
    b.   opponent-process theory.
    c.   localization theory.
    d.   rod-cone correspondence theory.

3.7   Lisa heard her name called in a large crowd and she turned immediately in the direction of the person
    calling her name. She had used the phenomenon of
    a.   perceptual constancy.
    b.   sound localization.
    c.   place theory.
    d.   frequency theory.

3.8   Someone who is following gate-control theory would make which suggestion to a
    person who has just scraped a finger?
    a.   Rub the back of the hand vigorously.
    b.   Take two aspirin and call me later.
    c.   Close your eyes and concentrate on the pain.
    d.   Let me hypnotize you into feeling no pain.

3.9   When a person's culture emphasizes the stoical acceptance of pain, a person is likely
        to respond by
        a.   overacting and responding excessively to pain.
        b.   enjoying pain, and inflicting it on others.
        c.   becoming able to tolerate high levels of pain silently.
        d.   making no change; this will not affect one's perception of pain.

3.10   When a police officer asks a suspected drunk driver "How many fingers do you
        see?" it is a test of vision. When the officer asks the driver to touch his finger to
        the tip of his nose with his eyes closed, which sense is being tested?
        a.   kinesthesis
        b.   olfaction
        c.   gustation
        d.   orientation

3.11   Our tendency to divide the perceptual world into two distinct parts is called
        a.   attentional grouping.
        b.   conscious-unconscious.
        c.   perceptual division.
        d.   figure-ground.

3.12   Even though the image of an object on the retina may change, our perception of that object does not
        change due to
        a.   brightness constancy.
        b.   shape constancy.
        c.   continuation constancy.
        d.   closure constancy.

3.13   Psychologists refer to illusions as
        a.   incorrect perceptions.
        b.   attentional deficits.
        c.   cognitive restructures.
        d.   enhanced perceptions.

3.14   When we are processing information about the world, if we let our expectations affect our perceptions, we
        are using the
        a.   bottom-up approach.
        b.   top-down approach.
        c.   attributional approach.
        d.   perceptual processing approach.

3.15   Convergence and retinal disparity are examples of
        a.   monocular cues used for perception of movement.
        b.   monocular cues used for perception of depth.
        c.   binocular cues used for perception of movement.
        d.   binocular cues used for perception of depth.

3.16   The definition of perception involves
        a.   transduction.
        b.   interpretation.
        c.   simplicity.
        d.   direct sensation.

3.17   Determining the lowest level of illumination that can be detected at least half of the
       time a light is presented is an example of determining a(n) _____ threshold.
       a.   psi
       b.   petite
       c.   absolute
       d.   difference

3.18   The sensory receptors in the eye are found in the
       a.   retina.
       b.   cochlea.
       c.   ganglion cells.
       d.   cornea.

3.19   The theory that holds that there are six cells that play a role in color vision is
       a.   trichromatic theory.
       b.   opponent process theory.
       c.   signal detection theory.
       d.   dark adaptation theory.

3.20   The characteristic of a sound that is described as being high or low is called
       a.   pitch.
       b.   loudness.
       c.   amplitude.
       d.   timbre.

3.21   Which of the following is **not** a basic taste for humans?
       a.   mint
       b.   bitter
       c.   salt
       d.   sweet

3.22   The process of _____ is described as the way in which we select, organize, and interpret sensory input
       to achieve a grasp of our surroundings.
       a.   sensation
       b.   attention
       c.   perception
       d.   kinesthesia

3.23   Size-distance invariance and the use of relative size are used to explain
       a.   the law of proximity.
       b.   shape constancy.
       c.   size constancy.
       d.   closure.

3.24   The illusion in which two equal lines appear to be of different lengths if they
       have different arrows attached to their ends is called the _____ illusion.
       a.   Muller-Lyer
       b.   Ponzo
       c.   railroad
       d.   Poggendorf

3.25   The ability to foretell future events is called
       a.   clairvoyance.
       b.   telepathy.
       c.   precognition.
       d.   psychokinesis.

Chapter 3 - Practice Test Answer Justifications

3.1   Detection is to interpretation as
    a.   This answer is incorrect because assigned threshold is not relevant to this question. Review page 85 in your textbook.
    b.   This answer is incorrect because assigned threshold is not relevant to this question. Review page 85 in your textbook.
    c.   For more information, see page 85 in your textbook.
    d.   This answer is incorrect because perception involves interpretation and sensation involves detection. Review page 85 in your textbook.

3.2   The smallest magnitude of a stimulus that can be readily discriminated from no stimulus at all 50% of the time is called
    a.   For more information, see page 87 in your textbook.
    b.   This answer is incorrect because extrasensory threshold is not applicable. Review page 87 in your textbook.
    c.   This answer is incorrect because difference threshold is concerned with the difference between two stimuli. Review page 87 in your textbook.
    d.   This answer is incorrect because petite threshold is not applicable. Review page 87 in your textbook.

3.3   An experimenter has you compare the temperature of water in two different containers. She asks you if they feel the same or different. She is probably trying to determine your
    a.   This answer is incorrect because subliminal threshold is not applicable. Review page 89 in your textbook.
    b.   This answer is incorrect because absolute threshold is concerned with one stimulus. Review page 89 in your textbook.
    c.   For more information, see page 89 in your textbook.
    d.   This answer is incorrect because frequency threshold is not applicable. Review page 89 in your textbook.

3.4   The rods in the retina are light-sensitive receptors used primarily for
    a.   This answer is incorrect because cones serve this function. Review page 93 in your textbook.
    b.   This answer is incorrect because the lens of the eye serves this purpose. Review page 93 in your textbook.
    c.   For more information, see page 93 in your textbook.
    d.   This answer is incorrect because the cones serve this function. Review page 93 in your textbook.

3.5   The saccadic movements of good readers tend to be
    a.   This answer is incorrect because these types of movements would be characteristic of poor readers. Review page 95 in your textbook.
    b.   This answer is incorrect because good readers would have few backward movements. Review page 95 in your textbook.
    c.   This answer is incorrect because such movements would be characteristic of poor readers. Review page 95 in your textbook.
    d.   For more information, see page 95 in your textbook.

3.6   Negative afterimages are more effectively explained by
    a.   This answer is incorrect because trichromatic theory emphasizes maximally sensitive cones and afterimages involve minimally sensitive cones. Review page 96 in your textbook.
    b.   For more information, see page 96 in your textbook.
    c.   This answer is incorrect because localization theory is not applicable to this situation. Review page 96 in your textbook.
    d.   This answer is incorrect because this theory is not applicable to this question. Review page 96 in your textbook.

3.7   Lisa heard her name called in a large crowd and she turned immediately in the direction of the person calling her name. She had used the phenomenon of
   a.   This answer is incorrect because perceptual constancy involves other senses, not just hearing. Review page 101 in your textbook.
   b.   For more information, see page 101 in your textbook.
   c.   This answer is incorrect because place theory is an attempt to explain the pitch of a sound. Review page 101 in your textbook.
   d.   This answer is incorrect because frequency theory is an attempt to explain the pitch of a sound. Review page 101 in your textbook.

3.8   Someone who is following gate-control theory would make which suggestion to a person who has just scraped a finger?
   a.   For more information, see page 105 in your textbook.
   b.   This answer is incorrect because such action involves medication and is not applicable. Review page 105 in your textbook.
   c.   This answer is incorrect because such activity would tend to increase the attention given to the pain. Review page 105 in your textbook.
   d.   This answer is incorrect because such activity is not applicable to this question. Review page 105 in your textbook.

3.9   When a person's culture emphasizes the stoical acceptance of pain, a person is likely to respond by
   a.   This answer is incorrect because this answer is the opposite reaction expressed in the question. Review page 105 in your textbook.
   b.   This answer is incorrect because such action involves abnormal behavior. Review page 105 in your textbook.
   c.   For more information, see page 105 in your textbook.
   d.   This answer is incorrect because culture does have an effect on the perception of pain. Review page 105 in your textbook.

3.10 When a police officer ask a suspected drunk driver "How many fingers do you see?" it is a test of vision. When the officer asks the driver to touch his finger to the tip of his nose with his eyes closed, which sense is being tested?
   a.   For more information, see page 109 in your textbook.
   b.   This answer is incorrect because olfaction involves the sense of smell. Review page 109 in your textbook.
   c.   This answer is incorrect because gustation involves the sense of taste. Review page 109 in your textbook.
   d.   This answer is incorrect because orientation involves attention to stimuli. Review page 109 in your textbook.

3.11 Our tendency to divide the perceptual world into two distinct parts is called
   a.   This answer is incorrect because attentional groups involves the restricted process of attention. Review page 113 in your textbook.
   b.   This answer is incorrect because the unconscious end of this continuum would not involve the perceptual world. Review page 113 in your textbook.
   c.   This answer is incorrect because perceptual division is not applicable to this question. Review page 113 in your textbook.
   d.   For more information, see page 113 in your textbook.

3.12 Even though the image of an object on the retina may change, our perception of that object does not change due to
   a.   This answer is incorrect because this constancy involves the perception of brightness, not the changing of the retinal image. Review page 115 in your textbook.
   b.   For more information, see page 115 in your textbook.
   c.   This answer is incorrect because this constancy does not exist. Review page 115 in your textbook.
   d.   This answer is incorrect because this constancy does not exist. Review page 115 in your textbook.

3.13   Psychologists refer to illusions as
   a.   For more information, see page 116 in your textbook.
   b.   This answer is incorrect because attentional deficits can be overridden by illusions. Review page 116 in your textbook.
   c.   This answer is incorrect because cognitive restructures implies reorganizing of our cognitive structure, which does not occur with an illusion. Review page 116 in your textbook.
   d.   This answer is incorrect because enhanced perceptions are not applicable. Review page 116 in your textbook.

3.14   When we are processing information about the world, if we let our expectations affect our perceptions, we are using the
   a.   This answer is incorrect because such an approach suggests that pattern recognition derives from simpler abilities. Review page 119 in your textbook.
   b.   For more information, see page 119 in your textbook.
   c.   This answer is incorrect because such an approach involves trying to find cause for behavior. Review page 119 in your textbook.
   d.   This answer is incorrect because this approach is too broad for this question. Review page 119 in your textbook.

3.15   Convergence and retinal disparity are examples of
   a.   This answer is incorrect because these are two binocular cues. Review page 120 in your textbook.
   b.   This answer is incorrect because these are two binocular cues. Review page 120 in your textbook.
   c.   This answer is incorrect because these are cues for depth. Review page 120 in your textbook.
   d.   For more information, see page 120 in your textbook.

3.16   The definition of perception involves
   a.   This answer is incorrect because transduction involves changing physical energy into electrical signals. Review page 85 in your textbook.
   b.   For more information, see page 85 in your textbook.
   c.   This answer is incorrect because simplicity is not part of the definition. Review page 85 in your textbook.
   d.   This answer is incorrect because direct sensation is not involved in the definition. Review page 85 in your textbook.

3.17   Determining the lowest level of illumination that can be detected at least half of the time a light is presented is an example of determining a(n) _____ threshold.
   a.   This answer is incorrect because psi is considered to be a paranormal phenomenon. Review page 87 in your textbook.
   b.   This answer is incorrect because petite is usually not associated with a threshold. Review page 87 in your textbook.
   c.   For more information, see page 87 in your textbook.
   d.   This answer is incorrect because difference is associated with a just noticeable difference. Review page 87 in your textbook.

3.18   The sensory receptors in the eye are found in the
   a.   For more information, see page 93 in your textbook.
   b.   This answer is incorrect because the cochlea is part of the inner ear. Review page 93 in your textbook.
   c.   This answer is incorrect because ganglion cells are retinal cells, but not receptor cells. Review page 93 in your textbook.
   d.   This answer is incorrect because the cornea is on the outside of the eye and is not a sensory receptor. Review page 93 in your textbook.

3.19   The theory that holds that there are six cells that play a role in color vision is
   a.   This answer is incorrect because trichromatic theory specifies that we have three different types of cells. Review page 96 in your textbook.
   b.   For more information, see page 96 in your textbook.
   c.   This answer is incorrect because signal detection theory is not directly involved in color vision. Review page 96 in your textbook.
   d.   This answer is incorrect because dark adaptation theory is not directly involved in color vision. Review page 96 in your textbook..

3.20   The characteristic of a sound that is described as being high or low is called
   a.   For more information, see page 99 in your textbook.
   b.   This answer is incorrect because loudness depends on the height, not the frequency, of the sound wave. Review page 99 in your textbook..
   c.   This answer is incorrect because amplitude is related to height of the sound wave, and loudness. Review page 99 in your textbook.
   d.   This answer is incorrect because timbre is related to the quality of a sound. Review page 99 in your textbook.

3.21   Which of the following is **not** a basic taste for humans?
   a.   For more information, see page 107 in your textbook.
   b.   This answer is incorrect because bitter is a basic taste. Review page 107 in your textbook.
   c.   This answer is incorrect because salt is a basic taste. Review page 107 in your textbook.
   d.   This answer is incorrect because sweet is a basic taste. Review page 107 in your textbook.

3.22   The process of _____ is described as the way in which we select, organize, and interpret sensory input to achieve a grasp of our surroundings.
   a.   This answer is incorrect because sensation is the process of reception of stimulation. Review page 112 in your textbook.
   b.   This answer is incorrect because attention is related to selection of stimuli only. Review page 112 in your textbook.
   c.   For more information, see page 112 in your textbook.
   d.   This answer is incorrect because kinesthesia is involved in movement and balance specifically. Review page 112 in your textbook.

3.23   Size-distance invariance and the use of relative size are used to explain
   a.   This answer is incorrect because the law of proximity involves stimuli that are close to one another. Review page 115 in your textbook.
   b.   This answer is incorrect because shape constancy does not depend upon size. Review page 115 in your textbook.
   c.   For more information, see page 115 in your textbook.
   d.   This answer is incorrect because closure involves completing incomplete stimuli, not size. Review page 115 in your textbook.

3.24   The illusion in which two equal lines appear to be of different lengths if they have different arrows attached to their ends is called the _____ illusion.
   a.   For more information, see page 117 in your textbook.
   b.   This answer is incorrect because the Ponzo illusion slanted lines. Review page 117 in your textbook.
   c.   This answer is incorrect because the railroad illusion involves slanted lines. Review page 117 in your textbook.
   d.   This answer is incorrect because the Poggendorf illusion involves slanted lines. Review page 117 in your textbook.

3.25   The ability to foretell future events is called

    a.   This answer is incorrect because clairvoyance involves perceiving stimuli that do not directly stimulate a sense organ. Review page 123 in your textbook.

    b.   This answer is incorrect because telepathy involves transfer of thought from one individual to another. Review page 123 in your textbook.

    c.   For more information, see page 123 in your textbook.

    d.   This answer is incorrect because psychokinesis involves the ability to affect the physical world through thought. Review page 123 in your textbook.

Chapter 3 - Practice Test Answers

Question	Answer
3.1	c
3.2	a
3.3	c
3.4	c
3.5	d
3.6	b
3.7	b
3.8	a
3.9	c
3.10	a
3.11	d
3.12	b
3.13	a
3.14	b
3.15	d
3.16	b
3.17	c
3.18	a
3.19	b
3.20	a
3.21	a
3.22	c
3.23	c
3.24	a
3.25	c

Chapter 4 - Practice Test

4.1   Fluctuations in bodily processes and in consciousness over the course of a single day are known as
    a.   biological rhythms.
    b.   circadian rhythms.
    c.   recurring rhythms.
    d.   reverberating rhythms.

4.2   The pineal gland secretes a hormone known as _____ that seems to trigger hibernation in certain species and also plays a role in circadian rhythms.
    a.   epinephrine
    b.   adrenaline
    c.   endorphin
    d.   melatonin

4.3   Ralph has just flown on a jet from Los Angeles, California to Ithaca, New York. He would be expected to experience _____ due to jet lag.
    a.   a high degree of disruption
    b.   a moderate degree of disruption
    c.   a weak degree of disruption
    d.   no disruption

4.4   In the attentional state labeled _____, only one task at a time can be performed.
    a.   automatic processing
    b.   limited attention
    c.   attention deficit
    d.   controlled processing

4.5   Based upon EEG records, it appears that sleep can be divided into
    a.   four distinct stages
    b.   two distinct states
    c.   unlimited stages, depending upon the individual.
    d.   no distinct stages

4.6   The strongest result of depriving people of REM sleep is that the people begin to show
    a.   significant memory losses for their daily experiences.
    b.   major mood changes, including depression.
    c.   increased risks for infectious diseases.
    d.   more REM sleep the next few nights.

4.7   The sleep disorder characterized by walking in one's sleep is called
    a.   apnea.
    b.   narcolepsy.
    c.   somnambulism.
    d.   paradoxical sleep.

4.8   Lisa has been trying to quit smoking and occasionally has a dream that reveals that she has slipped into smoking. Such dreams are called
    a.   DAMIT dreams.
    b.   SHUCKS dreams.
    c.   AST dreams
    d.   HABIT dreams

4.9   If hypnotic effects exist, they appear to
       a.   occur in many different people.
       b.   occur in selected classes of people
       c.   occur in males only.
       d.   occur in females only.

4.10   There appears to be two primary views regarding the explanation of hypnosis - the _____ view and the
       _____ view.
       a.   neoclassic, perceptual
       b.   social-cognitive, neodissociation
       c.   cognitive, dissociation
       d.   classic, sensational

4.11   When one drug increases the tolerance for another drug, this process is called
       a.   addiction.
       b.   abuse.
       c.   dependence.
       d.   cross-tolerance.

4.12   Which statement best reflects the learning perspective of drug use?
       a.   People use drugs as rewards for "good" behavior.
       b.   People take drugs to fit in with a social group.
       c.   People use drugs to avoid unconscious anxiety
       d.   People take drugs as an automatic behavior

4.13   In relatively large doses, alcohol acts as a
       a.   stimulant.
       b.   depressant.
       c.   psychedelic.
       d.   barbiturate.

4.14   Barbiturate is to cocaine as
       a.   opiate is to hallucinogen.
       b.   hallucinogen is to opiate.
       c.   depressant is to stimulant.
       d.   stimulant is to depressant.

4.15   The _____ suggests that marijuana use linked to the use of other, more dangerous drugs.
       a.   amotivational syndrome
       b.   higher use syndrome
       c.   gateway hypothesis
       d.   contingency hypothesis

4.16   Lisa recently took a test and found out that she was a "night" person. What time of day would you advise
       her to take classes?
       a.   morning classes
       b.   afternoon classes
       c.   all day Saturday classes
       d.   it really does not matter

4.17   What type of processing are you demonstrating when you are watching a basketball
       game on television and listening to your favorite song on your stereo?
       a.   controlled
       b.   latent
       c.   automatic
       d.   manifest

4.18 Assuming you are fully awake and alert, your EEG pattern would probably contain many
   a. delta waves.
   b. alpha waves.
   c. beta waves.
   d. theta waves.

4.19 When an individual experiences such severe disturbances in sleep such that slow-wave sleep and REM sleep disappears, that individual is said to have
   a. somnambulism.
   b. narcolepsy.
   c. fatal familial insomnia.
   d. cataplasia.

4.20 Cognitive events, often vivid but disconnected, that occur during sleep are called
   a. hypnotic states.
   b. night terrors.
   c. dreams.
   d. repressions.

4.21 An interaction between two individuals in which one induces changes in behavior in the other through suggestions is called
   a. role playing.
   b. therapy.
   c. hypnosis.
   d. dreaming.

4.22 As a result of taking barbiturates, higher doses of alcohol are needed to produce alcohol's euphoric effects. This is an example of
   a. psychological dependency.
   b. cross tolerance.
   c. alcohol withdrawal.
   d. drug transfer.

4.23 Alcohol is classified as
   a. a depressant.
   b. a stimulant.
   c. an opiate.
   d. a hallucinogen.

4.24 Drugs that generate sensory perceptions for which there are no external stimuli are
   a. stimulants.
   b. depressants.
   c. hallucinogens.
   d. endorphins.

4.25 Marijuana is a widely used _____ drug.
   a. opiate
   b. sedative
   c. stimulant
   d. psychedelic

Chapter 4 - Practice Test Answer Justifications

4.1   Fluctuations in bodily processes and in consciousness over the course of a single day are known as
   a.   This answer is incorrect because biological rhythms is a general term describing fluctuations. Review page 131 in your textbook.
   b.   For more information, see page 131 in your textbook.
   c.   This answer is incorrect because recurring rhythms is not applicable. Review page 131 in your textbook.
   d.   This answer is incorrect because reverberating rhythms is not applicable. Review page 131 in your textbook.

4.2   The pineal gland secretes a hormone known as _____ that seems to trigger hibernation in certain species and also plays a role in circadian rhythms.
   a.   This answer is incorrect because epinephrine is secreted by the adrenal glands. Review page 132 in your textbook.
   b.   This answer is incorrect because adrenaline is secreted by the adrenal glands. Review page 132 in your textbook.
   c.   This answer is incorrect because an endorphin is a neurotransmitter produced by the brain. Review page 132 in your textbook.
   d.   For more information, see page 132 in your textbook.

4.3   Ralph has just flown on a jet from Los Angeles, California to Ithaca, New York. He would be expected to experience _____ due to jet lag.
   a.   For more information, see page 133 in your textbook.
   b.   This answer is incorrect because flying to a later time zone creates greater disruption. Review page 133 in your textbook.
   c.   This answer is incorrect because flying to a later time zone creates greater disruption. Review page 133 in your textbook.
   d.   This answer is incorrect because changing time zones will create some disruption. Review page 133 in your textbook.

4.4   In the attentional state labeled _____, only one task at a time can be performed.
   a.   This answer is incorrect because automatic processing enables one to work on several different tasks at the same time. Review page 137 in your textbook.
   b.   This answer is incorrect because the amount of attention is not relevant to this question. Review page 137 in your textbook.
   c.   This answer is incorrect because the level of attention is not relevant to this question. Review page 137 in your textbook.
   d.   For more information, see page 137 in your textbook.

4.5   Based upon EEG records, it appears that sleep can be divided into
   a.   For more information, see page 143 in your textbook.
   b.   This answer is incorrect because there are four distinct states in sleep. Review page 143 in your textbook.
   c.   This answer is incorrect because the research indicates four distinct stages, regardless of the individual. Review page 143 in your textbook.
   d.   This answer is incorrect because there are distinct stages. Review page 143 in your textbook.

4.6   The strongest result of depriving people of REM sleep is that the people begin to show
   a.   This answer is incorrect because there does not seem to be significant memory losses for most individuals. Review page 145 in your textbook.
   b.   This answer is incorrect because the research indicates no significant level of depression. Review page 145 in your textbook.
   c.   This answer is incorrect because infectious diseases would require having contact with another individual, which does not always occur. Review page 145 in your textbook.
   d.   For more information, see page 145 in your textbook.

4.7 The sleep disorder characterized by walking in one's sleep is called
   a. This answer is incorrect because apnea is a sleep disorder that involves stopping of breathing. Review page 147 in your textbook.
   b. This answer is incorrect because narcolepsy involves falling asleep at odd and inappropriate times. Review page 147 in your textbook.
   c. For more information, see page 147 in your textbook.
   d. This answer is incorrect because paradoxical sleep involves REM sleep. Review page 147 in your textbook.

4.8 Lisa has been trying to quit smoking and occasionally has a dream that reveals that she has slipped into smoking. Such dreams are called
   a. For more information, see page 149 in your textbook.
   b. This answer is incorrect because there are no such dreams. Review page 149 in your textbook.
   c. This answer is incorrect because there are no such dreams. Review page 149 in your textbook.
   d. This answer is incorrect because there are no such dreams. Review page 149 in your textbook.

4.9 If hypnotic effects exist, they appear to
   a. This answer is incorrect because such effects appear to occur in a select, small group of people (primarily about 15% of adults). Review page 151 in your textbook.
   b. For more information, see page 151 in your textbook.
   c. This answer is incorrect because such effects occur in both genders. Review page 151 in your textbook.
   d. This answer is incorrect because such effects occur in both genders. Review page 151 in your textbook.

4.10 There appears to be two primary views regarding the explanation of hypnosis - the _____ view and the _____ view.
   a. This answer is incorrect because these two responses are not applicable to this question. Review page 151 in your textbook.
   b. For more information, see page 151 in your textbook.
   c. This answer is incorrect because these two responses are not applicable to this question. Review page 151 in your textbook.
   d. This answer is incorrect because these two responses are not applicable to this question. Review page 151 in your textbook.

4.11 When one drug increases the tolerance for another drug, this process is called
   a. This answer is incorrect because addiction involves a dependence on a drug. Review page 155 in your textbook.
   b. This answer is incorrect because abuse may not be relevant to tolerance. Review page 155 in your textbook.
   c. This answer is incorrect because dependence is potentially applicable to all drugs. Review page 155 in your textbook.
   d. For more information, see page 155 in your textbook.

4.12 Which statement best reflects the learning perspective of drug use?
   a. For more information, see page 156 in your textbook.
   b. This answer is incorrect because it reflects the social perspective of drug use. Review page 156 in your textbook.
   c. This answer is incorrect because it reflects the psychodynamic perspective of drug use. Review page 156 in your textbook.
   d. This answer is incorrect because it reflects the cognitive perspective of drug use. Review page 156 in your textbook.

4.13   In relatively large doses, alcohol acts as a
a.   This answer is incorrect because in small doses alcohol may be perceived as a stimulant, but not in large doses. Review page 157 in your textbook.
b.   For more information, see page 157 in your textbook.
c.   This answer is incorrect because alcohol use does not result in the extreme alterations of sensory perceptions. Review page 157 in your textbook.
d.   This answer is incorrect because barbiturates represent a second, and different, class of depressants. Review page 157 in your textbook.

4.14   Barbiturate is to cocaine as
a.   This answer is incorrect because an opiate and a hallucinogen do not have opposite effects. Review page 158 in your textbook.
b.   This answer is incorrect because a hallucinogen does not have an opposite effect to that of an opiate. Review page 158 in your textbook.
c.   For more information, see page 157 in your textbook.
d.   This answer is incorrect because a barbiturate is a depressant and cocaine is a stimulant. Review page 157 in your textbook.

4.15   The _____ suggests that marijuana use linked to the use of other, more dangerous drugs.
a.   This answer is incorrect because there is no specific syndrome that results in such connection. Review page 161 in your textbook.
b.   This answer is incorrect because this syndrome does not exist. Review page 161 in your textbook.
c.   For more information, see page 161 in your textbook.
d.   This answer is incorrect because using other dangerous drugs is not dependent upon the use of marijuana. Review page 161 in your textbook.

4.16   Lisa recently took a test and found out that she was a "night" person. What time of day would you advise her to take classes?
a.   This answer is incorrect because morning classes would not capitalize on her high activity level time. Review page 132 in your textbook.
b.   For more information, see page 132 in your textbook.
c.   This answer is incorrect because all day Saturday classes would require her to be alert during the morning, the time at which she is least alert. Review page 132 in your textbook.
d.   This answer is incorrect because if a person wants to capitalize on the period of time when someone is most alert, it really does matter. Review page 132 in your textbook.

4.17   What type of processing are you demonstrating when you are watching a basketball game on television and listening to your favorite song on your stereo?
a.   This answer is incorrect because controlled processing would require effort to listen to one or the other. Review page 137 in your textbook.
b.   This answer is incorrect because latent processing is not relevant to this situation. Review page 137 in your textbook.
c.   For more information, see page 137 in your textbook.
d.   This answer is incorrect because manifest processing is not a relevant phenomenon. Review page 137 in your textbook.

4.18   Assuming you are fully awake and alert, your EEG pattern would probably contain many
a.   This answer is incorrect because delta waves occur during Stage 3 sleep. Review page 143 in your textbook.
b.   This answer is incorrect because alpha waves occur when a person enters a quiet resting state. Review page 143 your textbook.
c.   For more information, see page 143 in your textbook.
d.   This answer is incorrect because theta waves are present during REM sleep. Review page 143 your textbook.

4.19   When an individual experiences such severe disturbances in sleep such that slow-wave sleep and REM sleep disappears, that individual is said to have
a. This answer is incorrect because somnambulism involves sleepwalking. Review page 145 in your textbook.
b. This answer is incorrect because narcolepsy involves uncontrollable urges to sleep. Review page 145 in your textbook.
c. For more information, see page 145 in your textbook.
d. This answer is incorrect because cataplasia involves falling down without warning. Review page 145 in your textbook.

4.20   Cognitive events, often vivid but disconnected, that occur during sleep are called
a. This answer is incorrect because hypnotic states do not occur during sleep. Review page 148 in your textbook.
b. This answer is incorrect because night terrors have feelings of fear involved. Review page 148 in your textbook.
c. For more information, see page 148 in your textbook.
d. This answer is incorrect because repressions are psychoanalytic concepts and may not be involved in sleep. Review page 148 in your textbook.

4.21   An interaction between two individuals in which one induces changes in behavior in the other through suggestions is called
a. This answer is incorrect because role playing does not necessarily involve two individuals, nor suggestions. Review page 150 in your textbook.
b. This answer is incorrect because depending upon the type therapy suggestions may not be involved. Review page 150 in your textbook.
c. For more information, see page 150 in your textbook.
d. This answer is incorrect because dreaming does not involve another person directly. Review page 150 in your textbook.

4.22   As a result of taking barbiturates, higher doses of alcohol are needed to produce alcohol's euphoric effects. This is an example of
a. This answer is incorrect because psychological dependency could be to either drug. Review page 155 in your textbook.
b. For more information, see page 155 in your textbook.
c. This answer is incorrect because alcohol withdrawal is not involved in this situation. Review page 155 in your textbook.
d. This answer is incorrect because drug transfer is not relevant to this situation. Review page 155 in your textbook.

4.23   Alcohol is classified as
a. For more information, see page 157 in your textbook.
b. This answer is incorrect because, in small doses, alcohol can induce feelings of excitement, but overall, alcohol is a depressant. Review page 157 in your textbook.
c. This answer is incorrect because alcohol is not classified as an opiate. Review page 157 in your textbook.
d. This answer is incorrect because alcohol does not produce the same effects as a hallucinogen. Review page 157 in your textbook.

4.24   Drugs that generate sensory perceptions for which there are no external stimuli are
a. This answer is incorrect because stimulants have a precipitating event for their effect. Review page 159 in your textbook.
b. This answer is incorrect because depressants have a precipitating event for their effect. Review page 159 in your textbook..
c. For more information, see page 159 in your textbook.
d. This answer is incorrect because endorphins are stimulated by some event. Review page 159 in your textbook.

4.25　Marijuana is a widely used _____ drug.

    a.　This answer is incorrect because marijuana is not classed as an opiate. Review page 160 in your textbook.

    b.　This answer is incorrect because marijuana is not classed as a sedative. Review page 160 in your textbook.

    c.　This answer is incorrect because marijuana is not classed as a stimulant. Review page 160 in your textbook.

    d.　For more information, see page 160 in your textbook.

Chapter 5 - Practice Test Answers

Question	Answer
5.1	b
5.2	d
5.3	a
5.4	d
5.5	a
5.6	d
5.7	c
5.8	a
5.9	b
5.10	b
5.11	d
5.12	a
5.13	b
5.14	c
5.15	c
5.16	b
5.17	c
5.18	c
5.19	c
5.20	c
5.21	c
5.22	b
5.23	a
5.24	c
5.25	d

Chapter 5 - Practice Test

5.1 A relatively permanent change in behavior, or behavior potential, due to experience, is called
    a. learning.
    b. pseudoconditioning.
    c. response substitution.
    d. behavioral potentiation.

5.2 In classical conditioning, the stimulus that comes to elicit a response as a result of pairing with another stimulus is called the
    a. generalized stimulus.
    b. neutral stimulus.
    c. conditioned stimulus.
    d. unconditioned stimulus.

5.3 Research suggests that _____ is generally the most effective method for establishing a conditioned response.
    a. trace conditioning
    b. delayed conditioning
    c. simultaneous conditioning
    d. backward conditioning

5.4 Which of the following is **not** one of the factors that affects classical conditioning?
    a. increase in intensity of the stimuli
    b. familiarity of the stimuli
    c. temporal arrangement of the CS-UCS pairing
    d. cognitive characteristics of the stimuli

5.5 Stimulus generalization
    a. is the tendency of stimuli dissimilar to the conditioned stimulus to produce conditioned responses.
    b. is identical to stimulus discrimination.
    c. is the tendency of stimuli similar to the conditioned stimulus to produce conditioned responses.
    d. occurs when the US and CS are no longer paired.

5.6 The tendency of some species to acquire some forms of conditioning less readily than other species is called
    a. biological constraints on learning.
    b. conditioned taste aversion.
    c. species specific conditioning.
    d. one-trial leaning.

5.7 After conditioning, when the CS occurs, an individual expects the UCS to occur, indicating a
    a. conative process.
    b. behavioral process.
    c. conditioning process.
    d. cognitive process.

5.8 Learning an association between particular behaviors and their consequences occurs in
    a. operant conditioning.
    b. classical conditioning.
    c. conditioned taste aversion.
    d. blocking.

5.9 In operant conditioning, procedures that strengthen behaviors are termed
a. reinforcements.
b. consequences.
c. shaping.
d. chaining.

5.10 Negative reinforcement is to punishment as
a. response decrease is to response increase.
b. response increase is to response decrease.
c. response decrease is to response decrease.
d. response increase is to response increase.

5.11 Complex sequences of behavior, such as a dolphin jumping through a hoop, is produced through a process called
a. masking.
b. chaining.
c. generalization.
d. blocking.

5.12 The schedule where reinforcement occurs only after a constant number of responses is called
a. fixed interval schedule.
b. fixed contingency schedule.
c. fixed ratio schedule.
d. fixed blocking schedule.

5.13 One of the most impressive uses of operant techniques in the area of teaching involves the use of
a. computer-assisted instruction.
b. personalized instruction.
c. biofeedback.
d. multiple-baseline design.

5.14 Children who watched an adult attack a doll were more likely to attack the doll later on. This is evidence for the importance of
a. classical conditioning.
b. maturational development.
c. stimulus generalization.
d. observational learning.

5.15 Which of the following influences observational learning?
a. flooding
b. biofeedback
c. desensitization
d. motivation

5.16 Operant and classical conditioning are forms of
a. vicarious learning.
b. maturational changes.
c. learning.
d. sensitization.

5.17   The response that is learned as a result of classical conditioning is called the
       a.   operant response.
       b.   instrumental response.
       c.   conditioned response.
       d.   unconditioned response.

5.18   The tendency of stimuli similar to a conditioned stimulus to evoke a conditioned
       response is called
       a.   stimulus blocking.
       b.   spontaneous recovery.
       c.   stimulus discrimination.
       d.   stimulus generalization.

5.19   Conditioned taste aversions
       a.   are easy to extinguish.
       b.   require many CS-US pairings.
       c.   are difficult to extinguish.
       d.   occur with animals, but not with people.

5.20   Stimulus events or consequences that strengthen responses that precede them are called
       a.   operant stimuli.
       b.   unconditioned stimuli.
       c.   positive reinforcers.
       d.   omission stimuli.

5.21   A procedure by which the application or removal of a stimulus decreases the strength of a behavior is
       called
       a.   extinction.
       b.   reinforcement.
       c.   punishment.
       d.   spontaneous recovery.

5.22   The schedule that tends to produce a steady rate of responding without pauses is a
       a.   variable interval schedule.
       b.   fixed ratio schedule.
       c.   variable ratio schedule.
       d.   fixed interval schedule.

5.23   Stimuli that signal the availability of a reinforcer are called
       a.   unconditioned stimuli.
       b.   constraining stimuli.
       c.   discriminative stimuli.
       d.   omission stimuli.

5.24   If you are concerned that television viewers may acquire new ways to express
       aggression, then as a learning theorist you are most likely to be concerned with
       a.   observational learning.
       b.   blocking phenomenon.
       c.   systematic desensitization.
       d.   reinforcement schedules.

5.25 If you were starting a weight loss program, which of the following principles of learning would be of most importance to you?

a. spontaneous recovery
b. blocking
c. shaping
d. extinction

Chapter 5 - Practice Test Answer Justifications

5.1   A relatively permanent change in behavior, or behavior potential, due to experience, is called
   a.   For more information, see page 168 in your textbook.
   b.   This answer is incorrect because pseudoconditioning involves the appearance of conditioning when in fact conditioning does not occur. Review page 168 in your textbook.
   c.   This answer is incorrect because stimulus substitution involves replacing one stimulus with another, which would not necessarily involve learning. Review page 168 in your textbook.
   d.   This answer is incorrect because behavioral potentiation involves the potential for a behavior to occur. Review page 168 in your textbook.

5.2   In classical conditioning, the stimulus that comes to elicit a response as a result of pairing with another stimulus is called the
   a.   This answer is incorrect because this concept is not relevant to this question. Review page 171 in your textbook.
   b.   This answer is incorrect because a neutral stimulus does not elicit any specific response at the time it is paired with the unconditioned stimulus. Review page 171 in your textbook.
   c.   For more information, see page 171 in your textbook.
   d.   This answer is incorrect because an unconditioned stimulus elicits a response without pairing with another stimulus. Review page 171 in your textbook.

5.3   Research suggests that _____ is generally the most effective method for establishing a conditioned response.
   a.   This answer is incorrect because there may be too much time between presentation of the CS and UCS for conditioning to be established. Review page 173 in your textbook.
   b.   For more information, see page 173 in your textbook.
   c.   This answer is incorrect because there is no information presented to the organism that would be helpful in establishing the conditioned response. Review page 173 in your textbook.
   d.   This answer is incorrect because the UCS would have already been given, which would not help establish the CS-UCS connection. Review page 173 in your textbook.

5.4   Which of the following is **not** one of the factors that affects classical conditioning?
   a.   This answer is incorrect because increasing the intensity of a stimulus will decrease the time it takes to condition an organism. Review page 173 in your textbook.
   b.   This answer is incorrect because familiar stimuli do not usually signal something unusual is going to happen and will increase the time to condition an organism. Review page 173 in your textbook.
   c.   This answer is incorrect because CS-UCS time intervals definitely have an impact on classical conditioning. Review page 173 in your textbook.
   d.   For more information, see page 173 in your textbook.

5.5   Stimulus generalization:
   a.   This answer is incorrect because dissimilar stimuli have no connection to the conditioned stimulus. Review page 174 in your textbook.
   b.   This answer is incorrect because discrimination leads to different responses while generalization leads to similar responses. Review page 174 in your textbook.
   c.   For more information, see page 174 in your textbook.
   d.   This answer is incorrect because the lack of pairing would eventually lead to extinction. Review page 174 in your textbook.

5.6   The tendency of some species to acquire some forms of conditioning less readily than other species is called
    a.   For more information, see page 177 in your textbook.
    b.   This answer is incorrect because this aversion is not specific to one species. Review page 177 in your textbook.
    c.   This answer is incorrect because such conditioning implies that there is a specific type of conditioning for each type of species, and this implication is not accurate. Review page 177 in your textbook.
    d.   This answer is incorrect because one-trial learning is peculiar to conditioned taste aversion, and is not species related. Review page 177 in your textbook.

5.7   After conditioning, when the CS occurs, an individual expects the UCS to occur, indicating a
    a.   This answer is incorrect because conative implies emotion, which is not relevant. Review page 178 in your textbook.
    b.   This answer is incorrect because an expectation is not a behavior. Review page 178 in your textbook.
    c.   This answer is incorrect because conditioning has already occurred. Review page 178 in your textbook.
    d.   For more information, see page 178 in your textbook.

5.8   Learning an association between particular behaviors and their consequences occurs in
    a.   For more information, see page 182 in your textbook.
    b.   This answer is incorrect because classical conditioning involves learning associations between stimuli. Review page 182 in your textbook.
    c.   This answer is incorrect because this aversion is a specific type of classical conditioning. Review page 182 in your textbook.
    d.   This answer is incorrect because blocking involves classical conditioning. Review page 182 in your textbook.

5.9   In operant conditioning, procedures that strengthen behaviors are termed
    a.   For more information, see page 183 in your textbook.
    b.   This answer is incorrect because consequences could also weaken behaviors. Review page 183 in your textbook.
    c.   This answer is incorrect because shaping is a process involving the successive approximation of a final behavior. Review page 183 in your textbook.
    d.   This answer is incorrect because chaining is a process involving the arrangement of stimuli and reinforcements so that a series of behaviors will occur. Review page 183 in your textbook.

5.10   Negative reinforcement is to punishment as
    a.   This answer is incorrect because punishment decreases behavior. Review page 184 in your textbook.
    b.   For more information, see page 184 in your textbook.
    c.   This answer is incorrect because reinforcement increases behavior. Review page 184 in your textbook.
    d.   This answer is incorrect because punishment decreases behavior. Review page 184 in your textbook.

5.11   Complex sequences of behavior, such as a dolphin jumping through a hoop, is produced through a process called
    a.   This answer is incorrect because masking does not involve complex sequences of behavior. Review page 187 in your textbook.
    b.   For more information, see page 187 in your textbook.
    c.   This answer is incorrect because generalization does not necessarily involve complex sequences of behavior. Review page 187 in your textbook.
    d.   This answer is incorrect because blocking involves classical conditioning and not necessarily complex sequences of behavior. Review page 187 in your textbook.

5.12   The schedule where reinforcement occurs only after a constant number of responses is called
   a.   This answer is incorrect because an interval schedule involves time. Review page 191 in your textbook.
   b.   This answer is incorrect because interval schedule involves time. Review page 191 in your textbook.
   c.   For more information, see page 191 in your textbook.
   d.   This answer is incorrect because there is no schedule with this name. Review page 191 in your textbook.

5.13   One of the most impressive uses of operant techniques in the area of teaching involves the use of
   a.   For more information, see page 199 in your textbook.
   b.   This answer is incorrect because such instruction does not necessarily involve operant techniques. Review page 199 in your textbook.
   c.   This answer is incorrect because biofeedback involves bodily processes and the increase or decrease of these processes. Review page 199 in your textbook.
   d.   This answer is incorrect because this design is an experimental procedure to investigate cause of behavior. Review page 199 in your textbook.

5.14   Children who watched an adult attack a doll were more likely to attack the doll later on. This is evidence for the importance of
   a.   This answer is incorrect because there was no UCS-CS pairing. Review page 200 in your textbook.
   b.   This answer is incorrect because maturation is not relevant in this question. Review page 200 in your textbook.
   c.   This answer is incorrect because the stimuli were identical. Review page 200 in your textbook.
   d.   For more information, see page 200 in your textbook.

5.15   Which of the following influences observational learning?
   a.   This answer is incorrect because flooding is involved in therapy using classical conditioning. Review page 201 in your textbook.
   b.   This answer is incorrect because biofeedback involves physiological information from our bodies. Review page 201 in your textbook.
   c.   This answer is incorrect because desensitization is involved in therapy using classical conditioning. Review page 201 in your textbook.
   d.   For more information, see page 201 in your textbook.

5.16   Operant and classical conditioning are forms of
   a.   This answer is incorrect because vicarious learning is a form of learning. Review page 169 in your textbook.
   b.   This answer is incorrect because maturational changes involve biological, not conditioning changes. Review page 169 in your textbook.
   c.   For more information, see page 169 in your textbook.
   d.   This answer is incorrect because sensitization is not relevant to this situation. Review page 169 in your textbook.

5.17   The response that is learned as a result of classical conditioning is called the
   a.   This answer is incorrect because an operant response is related to operant conditioning. Review page 171 in your textbook.
   b.   This answer is incorrect because instrumental response is related to operant conditioning. Review page 171 in your textbook.
   c.   For more information, see page 171 in your textbook.
   d.   This answer is incorrect because an unconditioned response is the unlearned response. Review page 171 in your textbook.

5.18   The tendency of stimuli similar to a conditioned stimulus to evoke a conditioned
response is called
   a.   This answer is incorrect because stimulus blocking would prevent a response. Review page 174 in
        your textbook.
   b.   This answer is incorrect because spontaneous recovery occurs after a rest period and after the
        introduction of the conditioned stimulus. Review page 174 in your textbook.
   c.   This answer is incorrect because stimulus discrimination would involve different stimuli. Review page
        174 in your textbook.
   d.   For more information, see page 174 in your textbook.

5.19   Conditioned taste aversions
   a.   This answer is incorrect because taste aversion are not easy to extinguish because they may involve
        some survival value. Review page 177 in your textbook.
   b.   This answer is incorrect because the aversion is usually fairly severe and therefore does not require
        many CS-US pairings. Review page 177 in your textbook.
   c.   For more information, see page 177 in your textbook.
   d.   This answer is incorrect because taste aversions can occur with people undergoing cancer treatment.
        Review page 177 in your textbook.

5.20   Stimulus events or consequences that strengthen responses that precede them are called
   a.   This answer is incorrect because operant stimuli do not really exist except as setting occasions.
        Review page 183 in your textbook.
   b.   This answer is incorrect because an unconditioned stimuli occurs first.   Review page 183 in your
        textbook.
   c.   For more information, see page 183 in your textbook.
   d.   This answer is incorrect because omission stimuli is not relevant to this situation. Review page 183 in
        your textbook.

5.21   A procedure by which the application or removal of a stimulus decreases the strength of a behavior is
called
   a.   This answer is incorrect because extinction involves withholding a reinforcement. Review page 184 in
        your textbook.
   b.   This answer is incorrect because reinforcement involves strengthening a behavior. Review page 184
        in your textbook.
   c.   For more information, see page 184 in your textbook.
   d.   This answer is incorrect because spontaneous recovery involves the reappearance of a response upon
        reintroduction of the conditioned stimulus. Review page 184 in your textbook.

5.22   The schedule that tends to produce a steady rate of responding without pauses is a
   a.   For more information, see page 191 in your textbook.
   b.   This answer is incorrect because a fixed ratio schedule has pauses. Review page 191 in your textbook.
   c.   This answer is incorrect because the primary characteristic of a variable ratio schedule is a high rate of
        responding. A steady rate is not necessarily achieved regularly. Review page 191 in your textbook.
   d.   This answer is incorrect because a fixed interval schedule has regular and long pauses. Review page
        191 in your textbook.

5.23   Stimuli that signal the availability of a reinforcer are called
   a.   This answer is incorrect because unconditioned stimuli are involved in classical conditioning and not
        relevant to reinforcers. Review page 193 in your textbook.
   b.   This answer is incorrect because constraining stimuli are not phenomena. Review page 193 in your
        textbook.
   c.   For more information, see page 193 in your textbook.
   d.   This answer is incorrect because omission stimuli are not phenomena. Review page 193 in your
        textbook.

5.24   If you are concerned that television viewers may acquire new ways to express
aggression, then as a learning theorist you are most likely to be concerned with
   a.   For more information, see page 201 in your textbook.
   b.   This answer is incorrect because the blocking phenomenon is related to classical conditioning and the
impact of two stimuli on that paradigm. Review page 201 in your textbook.
   c.   This answer is incorrect because systematic desensitization is a process to reduce the fear someone has
of a situation or object. Review page 201 in your textbook.
   d.   This answer is incorrect because reinforcement schedules involve presentation of reinforcements at an
appropriate time and is not directly related to this situation. Review page 201 in your textbook.

5.25   If you were starting a weight loss program, which of the following principles of
learning would be of most importance to you?
   a.   This answer is incorrect because spontaneous recovery would mean that the original eating behavior
would return. Review page 205 in your textbook.
   b.   This answer is incorrect because blocking involves the combination of two stimuli in classical
conditioning. Review page 205 in your textbook.
   c.   For more information, see page 205 in your textbook.
   d.   This answer is incorrect because extinction would mean the elimination of all eating behavior, which
would be detrimental to your health. Review page 205 in your textbook.

Chapter 5 - Practice Test Answers

Question	Answer
5.1	a
5.2	c
5.3	b
5.4	d
5.5	c
5.6	a
5.7	d
5.8	a
5.9	a
5.10	b
5.11	b
5.12	c
5.13	a
5.14	d
5.15	d
5.16	c
5.17	c
5.18	d
5.19	c
5.20	c
5.21	c
5.22	a
5.23	c
5.24	a
5.25	c

Chapter 6 - Practice Test

6.1   The three tasks of memory are
    a. receiving, processing, storage.
    b. encoding, storage, retrieval.
    c. limiting, compression, processing.
    d. decoding, compression, retrieval.

6.2   The simplest memory system, sensory memory, holds
    a. cognitive schemas of sensory input for brief periods of time.
    b. limited representations of sensory input for extended periods of time.
    c. characterizations of sensory input for extended periods of time.
    d. representations of sensory input for brief periods of time.

6.3   Ralph has looked up a phone number to dial, but before he can dial the number, someone asks him the time. He has now forgotten the phone number, which he had stored in
    a. short-term memory.
    b. sensory memory.
    c. long-term memory.
    d. procedural memory.

6.4   Memory that holds vast amounts of information for very long periods of time is called
    a. sensory memory.
    b. long-term memory.
    c. prospective memory.
    d. perceptual memory.

6.5   The capacity of short-term memory is
    a. only one idea at any one time.
    b. essentially unlimited.
    c. around seven chunks.
    d. impossible to measure.

6.6   The process of combining separate pieces of information into units in short-term memory is called
    a. acoustical storage.
    b. chunking.
    c. reminiscence.
    d. paired-associate learning.

6.7   If Lisa asks Ralph if he knows how far it is from New York to London, she is assessing his
    a. semantic memory.
    b. episodic memory.
    c. procedural memory.
    d. prospective memory.

6.8   Which of the following involves shallow processing of information?
    a. determining if two words are synonyms
    b. deciding if a word fits in a sentence
    c. thinking of antonyms of a specific word
    d. counting the number of letters in a word

6.9   The fact that material learned in one environment is easier to remember in a similar environment than a
      very different environment is known as
      a.   emotion-dependent memory.
      b.   context-dependent memory.
      c.   state-dependent retrieval.
      d.   prototypical learning.

6.10 Ralph asked Lisa to think of a fruit and she said "Apple." This situation is an example of Lisa using
      a.   a hierarchal schema.
      b.   an organizational process.
      c.   a prototype.
      d.   an exemplar.

6.11 The process by which new information interferes with old information in memory is called
      a.   simultaneous interference.
      b.   proactive interference.
      c.   retroactive interference.
      d.   sequential interference.

6.12 Deciding whether memories come from external sources (our experiences) or from internal sources (our
      imagination) represent what is called
      a.   source monitoring.
      b.   reality monitoring.
      c.   schemas.
      d.   retrieval inhibition.

6.13 Recent research indicates that flashbulb memories are quite
      a.   general.
      b.   special.
      c.   accurate.
      d.   inaccurate.

6.14 Impairment of memory for events that occur after a serious operation is called
      a.   hyperamnesia.
      b.   distortion.
      c.   anterograde amnesia.
      d.   retrograde amnesia.

6.15 A modern view of memories suggests that they are represented
      a.   in multiple locations in the brain.
      b.   only in the hippocampus.
      c.   in the left hemisphere.
      d.   linearly in the thalamus and hypothalamus.

6.16 The way information is entered into memory is called
      a.   retrieval.
      b.   encoding.
      c.   storage.
      d.   programming.

6.17 The _____ is an analogy for a neural network model of memory.
      a.   computer
      b.   highway
      c.   sieve
      d.   spider web

6.18   Words at the end of a list are more easily remembered because they may be in
        a.   sensory memory.
        b.   long-term memory.
        c.   working memory.
        d.   procedural memory.

6.19   Lisa is taking a multiple choice exam, which is an example of a _____ task to measure memory.
        a.   sentence verification
        b.   redeintegrative
        c.   recognition
        d.   free recall

6.20   Being able to locate information that has previously been stored in memory refers to
        a.   encoding specificity.
        b.   elaborative rehearsal.
        c.   retrieval.
        d.   consolidation.

6.21   One of the most important factors in forgetting nonsense material appears to be
        a.   attention.
        b.   emotion.
        c.   interference.
        d.   decay.

6.22   A _____ is a cognitive framework that represents a person's knowledge and assumptions about the world.
        a.   construction
        b.   prototype
        c.   cognition
        d.   schema

6.23   The active elimination from consciousness of memories of experiences we find threatening is called
        a.   suppression.
        b.   repression.
        c.   regression.
        d.   sublimation.

6.24   Memory for events of our lives is called _____ memory.
        a.   semantic
        b.   procedural
        c.   personal
        d.   autobiographical

6.25   Impairment of memory for events that occur prior to severe head injury is called
        a.   anterograde amnesia.
        b.   retrograde amnesia.
        c.   hyperamnesia.
        d.   selective forgetting.

Chapter 6 - Practice Test Answer Justifications

6.1   The three tasks of memory are
a. This answer is incorrect because receiving and processing are not tasks of memory. Review page 211 in your textbook.
b. For more information, see page 211 in your textbook.
c. This answer is incorrect because none of these processes are tasks of memory. Review page 211 in your textbook.
d. This answer is incorrect because decoding and compression are not tasks of memory. Review page 211 in your textbook.

6.2   Memory that holds vast amounts of information for very long periods of time is called
a. This answer is incorrect because sensory memory involves temporary storage. Review page 212 in your textbook.
b. For more information, see page 212 in your textbook.
c. This answer is incorrect because this type of memory involves temporary storage. Review page 212 in your textbook.
d. This answer is incorrect because this type of memory does not involve long-term storage. Review page 212 in your textbook.

6.3   The simplest memory system, sensory memory, holds
a. This answer is incorrect because schemas are not involved in sensory memory. Review page 212 in your textbook.
b. This answer is incorrect because sensory memory does not involve extended periods of time. Review page 212 in your textbook.
c. This answer is incorrect because sensory memory does not involve extended periods of time. Review page 212 in your textbook.
d. For more information, see page 212 in your textbook.

6.4   Ralph has looked up a phone number to dial, but before he can dial the number, someone asks him the time. He has now forgotten the phone number, which he had stored in
a. For more information, see page 212 in your textbook.
b. This answer is incorrect because sensory memory would not involve processing the number. Review page 212 in your textbook.
c. This answer is incorrect because long-term memory would not be involved in such a temporary situation. Review page 212 in your textbook.
d. This answer is incorrect because procedural memory would involve how to dial the number, not the actual number. Review page 212 in your textbook.

6.5   The capacity of short-term memory is
a. This answer is incorrect because short-term memory has more capacity than one item. Review page 216 in your textbook.
b. This answer is incorrect because short-term memory is severely limited. Review page 216 in your textbook.
c. For more information, see page 216 in your textbook.
d. This answer is incorrect because Miller in the 1950s measured short-term memory. Review page 216 in your textbook.

6.6   The process of combining separate pieces of information into units in short-term memory is called
a. This answer is incorrect because such storage is limited to hearing processes. Review page 216 in your textbook.
b. For more information, see page 216 in your textbook.
c. This answer is incorrect because reminiscence involves remembering personal information, not necessarily discrete units. Review page 216 in your textbook.
d. This answer is incorrect because such learning involves learning one item of a pair and associating that item with another item. Review page 216 in your textbook.

6.7   If Lisa asks Ralph if he knows how far it is from New York to London, she is assessing his
        a.   For more information, see page 219 in your textbook.
        b.   This answer is incorrect because episodic memory involves specific episodes of our lives. Review
             page 219 in your textbook.
        c.   This answer is incorrect because procedural memory involves how to do a specific task. Review page
             219 in your textbook.
        d.   This answer is incorrect because prospective memory involves remembering what we are supposed to
             do. Review page 219 in your textbook.

6.8   Which of the following involves shallow processing of information?
        a.   This answer is incorrect because such an activity would involve a fairly deep level of processing.
             Review page 220 in your textbook.
        b.   This answer is incorrect because such an activity would involve a fairly deep level of processing.
             Review page 220 in your textbook.
        c.   This answer is incorrect because such an activity would involve a fairly deep level of processing.
             Review page 220 in your textbook.
        d.   For more information, see page 220 in your textbook.

6.9   The fact that material learned in one environment is easier to remember in a similar environment than a
        very different environment is known as
        a.   This answer is incorrect because emotion is not explicitly involved in this type of situation. Review
             page 220 in your textbook.
        b.   For more information, see page 220 in your textbook.
        c.   This answer is incorrect because such retrieval depends upon the internal state of the learner at the
             time the material was learned. Review page 220 in your textbook.
        d.   This answer is incorrect because prototypes do not necessarily involve the environment in which the
             material is learned. Review page 220 in your textbook.

6.10   Ralph asked Lisa to think of a fruit and she said "Apple." This situation is an example of Lisa using
        a.   This answer is incorrect because hierarchy is not relevant in this case, only an example. Review page
             222 in your textbook.
        b.   This answer is incorrect because a process is not being used, but recall of an example is being used.
             Review page 222 in your textbook.
        c.   This answer is incorrect because prototypes represent averages of categories. Review page 222 in
             your textbook.
        d.   For more information, see page 222 in your textbook.

6.11   The process by which new information interferes with old information in memory is called
        a.   This answer is incorrect because such interference would not consider the impact of time. Review
             page 225 in your textbook.
        b.   This answer is incorrect because in proactive interference, the old information interferes with the new
             information. Review page 225 in your textbook.
        c.   For more information, see page 225 in your textbook.
        d.   This answer is incorrect because such interference is simply describing the process of any type of
             interference. Review page 225 in your textbook.

6.12   Deciding whether memories come from external sources (our experiences) or from internal sources (our
        imagination) represent what is called
        a.   This answer is incorrect because such monitoring involves deciding the specific origin of a memory.
             Review page 228 in your textbook.
        b.   For more information, see page 228 in your textbook.
        c.   This answer is incorrect because schemas are cognitive organizations representing our knowledge of
             the world. Review page 228 in your textbook.
        d.   This answer is incorrect because retrieval inhibition involves blocking some information from recall
             by learning other items of information. Review page 228 in your textbook.

6.13   Recent research indicates that flashbulb memories are often quite
    a.   This answer is incorrect because these memories tend to be somewhat specific. Review page 234 in your textbook.
    b.   This answer is incorrect because the research indicates that these memories only seem to be special, but can be understood in terms that influence all autobiographical memories. Review page 234 in your textbook.
    c.   This answer is incorrect because they are no more accurate than other autobiographical memories. Review page 234 in your textbook.
    d.   For more information, see page 234 in your textbook.

6.14   Impairment of memory for events that occur after a serious operation is called
    a.   This answer is incorrect because such amnesia is not specific to when the amnesia-inducing event occurs. Review page 237 in your textbook.
    b.   This answer is incorrect because distortion is not specific enough for this situation. Review page 237 in your textbook.
    c.   For more information, see page 237 in your textbook.
    d.   This answer is incorrect because in this type of amnesia, the memory before an amnesia-inducing event is impaired. Review page 237 in your textbook.

6.15   A modern view of memories suggests that they are represented
    a.   For more information, see page 240 in your textbook.
    b.   This answer is incorrect because it appears that memories are not located in only one place, but throughout the brain. Review page 240 in your textbook.
    c.   This answer is incorrect because the right hemisphere is also involved in memory storage. Review page 240 in your textbook.
    d.   This answer is incorrect because these two structures are not central to memory storage. Review page 240 in your textbook.

6.16   The way information is entered into memory is called
    a.   This answer is incorrect because retrieval involves getting information from memory. Review page 211 in your textbook.
    b.   For more information, see page 211 in your textbook.
    c.   This answer is incorrect because storage involves retaining information in memory. Review page 211 in your textbook.
    d.   This answer is incorrect because programming is not relevant to this situation. Review page 211 in your textbook.

6.17   The _____ is an analogy for a neural network model of memory.
    a.   This answer is incorrect because a computer operates in a serial fashion. Review page 214 in your textbook.
    b.   This answer is incorrect because a highway operates in a linear fashion. Review page 214 in your textbook.
    c.   This answer is incorrect because a sieve retains nothing except big pieces. Review page 214 in your textbook.
    d.   For more information, see page 214 in your textbook.

6.18   Words at the end of a list are more easily remembered because they may be in
    a.   This answer is incorrect because information on a list would have been removed from sensory memory. Review page 215 in your textbook.
    b.   This answer is incorrect because long-term memory would be involved in the words at the beginning of the list. Review page 215 in your textbook.
    c.   For more information, see page 215 in your textbook.
    d.   This answer is incorrect because procedural memory involves how to do something, not words on a list. Review page 215 in your textbook.

6.19 Lisa is taking a multiple choice exam, which is an example of a _____ task to measure memory.
  a. This answer is incorrect because sentence verification is not relevant. Review page 218 in your textbook.
  b. This answer is incorrect because redeintegrative memory involves reconstructing a entire memory situation, which is not relevant. Review page 218 in your textbook.
  c. For more information, see page 218 in your textbook.
  d. This answer is incorrect because free recall would be more appropriate to an essay exam. Review page 218 in your textbook.

6.20 Being able to locate information that has previously been stored in memory refers to
  a. This answer is incorrect because encoding specificity would involve the placement of information into memory. Review page 220 in your textbook.
  b. This answer is incorrect because elaborative rehearsal involves moving information from working memory to long-term memory. Review page 220 in your textbook.
  c. For more information, see page 220 in your textbook.
  d. This answer is incorrect because consolidation involves a physiological process of putting information together to make sense with already stored information. Review page 220 in your textbook.

6.21 One of the most important factors in forgetting nonsense material appears to be
  a. This answer is incorrect because if attention was paid to the material, it would probably not be nonsense material and therefore not forgotten. Review page 225 in your textbook.
  b. This answer is incorrect because emotion does not play the most important role in dealing with nonsense material. Review page 225 in your textbook.
  c. For more information, see page 225 in your textbook.
  d. This answer is incorrect because decay is not a functional explanation of why forgetting occurs. Review page 225 in your textbook.

6.22 A _____ is a cognitive framework that represents a person's knowledge and assumptions about the world.
  a. This answer is incorrect because construction is not relevant to this situation. Review page 227 in your textbook.
  b. This answer is incorrect because a prototype is a model of something to be developed. Review page 227 in your textbook.
  c. This answer is incorrect because cognition is a much broader concept. Review page 227 in your textbook.
  d. For more information, see page 227 in your textbook.

6.23 The active elimination from consciousness of memories of experiences we find threatening is called
  a. This answer is incorrect because suppression does not necessarily eliminate the memory. Review page 230 in your textbook.
  b. For more information, see page 230 in your textbook.
  c. This answer is incorrect because regression involves going back to an earlier age. Review page 230 in your textbook.
  d. This answer is incorrect because sublimation is a defense mechanism and involves making the unacceptable acceptable. Review page 230 in your textbook.

6.24 Memory for events of our lives is called _____ memory.
  a. This answer is incorrect because semantic memory has to do with general, abstract material. Review page 232 in your textbook.
  b. This answer is incorrect because procedural memory has to do with how we do things. Review page 232 in your textbook.
  c. This answer is incorrect because personal memory is too general and applies to all types of memory. Review page 232 in your textbook.
  d. For more information, see page 232 in your textbook.

6.25   Impairment of memory for events that occur prior to severe head injury is called
   a.   This answer is incorrect because anterograde amnesia has to do with storage of information after the amnesia producing event. Review page 237 in your textbook.
   b.   For more information, see page 237 in your textbook.
   c.   This answer is incorrect because hyperamnesia is not a phenomenon. Review page 237 in your textbook.
   d.   This answer is incorrect because selective forgetting would mean that some events could be recalled, which is not the case. Review page 237 in your textbook.

Chapter 6 - Practice Test Answers

Question	Answer
6.1	b
6.2	b
6.3	d
6.4	a
6.5	c
6.6	b
6.7	a
6.8	d
6.9	b
6.10	d
6.11	c
6.12	b
6.13	d
6.14	c
6.15	a
6.16	b
6.17	d
6.18	c
6.19	c
6.20	c
6.21	c
6.22	d
6.23	b
6.24	d
6.25	b

Chapter 7 - Practice Test

7.1 Concepts that have no fixed and readily specified set of defining features are called
   a. expected utilities.
   b. availability heuristics.
   c. natural concepts.
   d. logical concepts.

7.2 Cognitive frameworks that represent our knowledge of and assumptions about the world are called
   a. visual images.
   b. sensory memories.
   c. schemas.
   d. concepts.

7.3 Our tendency to gather evidence that will confirm rather than refute a hypothesis we believe is called
   a. functional bias.
   b. confirmation bias.
   c. oversight bias.
   d. artificial intelligence.

7.4 The _____ involves the tendency to judge events as more predictable after they occur than before they occur.
   a. representative heuristic
   b. confirmation bias
   c. availability heuristic
   d. hindsight effect

7.5 Individuals sometimes take cognitive shortcuts, known as _____. in making decisions.
   a. syllogisms
   b. heuristics
   c. biases
   d. enhancements

7.6 According to the availability heuristic, the more easily we think of something, the more
   a. common we judge it to be.
   b. we like it.
   c. we dislike it.
   d. we understand it.

7.7 When alternatives are presented in terms of the losses that might result, most people are
   a. risk neutral.
   b. risk avoidant.
   c. risk averse.
   d. risk prone.

7.8 Lisa is using the process of _____ when she goes toward the interstate highway when she is trying to find a restaurant in an unfamiliar town.
   a. trial and error
   b. algorithm
   c. analogy
   d. means-end analysis

7.9 If an individual is asked to talk aloud while solving a problem, the experimenter is using
   a. verbal protocol processing.
   b. metacognitive processing.
   c. language structure processing.
   d. linguistic relativity processing.

7.10 A strong tendency to think of using objects only in ways they have been used before is called
   a. entrapment.
   b. escalation of commitment.
   c. confirmation bias.
   d. functional fixedness.

7.11 A child is learning to understand meaning of words, which indicates the mechanism of
   a. semantic development.
   b. phonological development.
   c. grammatical development
   d. syntactical development.

7.12 Young children use single word utterances that convey much meaning. These utterances are
   a. morphemes.
   b. phonemes.
   c. holophrases.
   d. syntax.

7.13 The view that language shapes thought is the
   a. operating principles theory.
   b. linguistic relativity hypothesis.
   c. social learning theory.
   d. innate mechanism hypothesis.

7.14 Washoe, a female chimp, was taught to use and understand almost 200 words in
   a. Analogy Sentence Language.
   b. Algorithm Sight Language.
   c. Animal Structured Language
   d. American Sign Language.

7.15 Which of the following was **not** mentioned as a guideline for increasing the chances that decisions will be good ones?
   a. Beware of availability.
   b. Question all anchors.
   c. Remain flexible.
   d. Select according to order.

7.16 The term _____ usually includes the mental activities associated with thought, decision making, language, and other higher mental processes.
   a. introspection
   b. reasoning
   c. thinking
   d. cognition

7.17   Which of the following may contain many different concepts?
        a. phonemes
        b. schemas
        c. morphemes
        d. prototypes

7.18   Cognitive activity that transforms information in order to reach specific conclusions
        is called
        a. semantic development.
        b. reasoning.
        c. artificial intelligence.
        d. syntax.

7.19   The process of choosing among various courses of action or alternatives is
        a. decision making.
        b. escalation of commitment.
        c. confirmation bias.
        d. hindsight effect.

7.20   After watching television shows of crime in a large U. S. city, many individuals overestimate
        the likelihood of becoming a crime victim. This can be explained on the basis of
        a. hindsight effect.
        b. availability heuristic.
        c. confirmation bias.
        d. representative heuristic.

7.21   The tendency to become trapped in bad decisions is known as
        a. framing.
        b. confirmation bias.
        c. overconfidence.
        d. escalation of commitment.

7.22   The tendency to stick with a familiar method of solving particular types of problems
        is called
        a. functional fixedness.
        b. availability heuristic.
        c. mental set.
        d. cognitive dissonance.

7.23   The study of how computers perform actions that in humans require cognitive abilities
        is called
        a. computer psychology.
        b. electronic cognition.
        c. artificial intelligence.
        d. mechanical thought.

7.24   A system of symbols, plus rules for combining them, used to communicate information is called
        a. intelligence.
        b. language.
        c. thinking.
        d. reasoning.

7.25   Language seems to be learned much more easily during early childhood than at any other time of life, a finding that is termed a(n)
a.   operating principle.
b.   linguistic phase.
c.   critical period.
d.   phonological loop.

Chapter 7 - Practice Test Answer Justifications

7.1   Concepts that have no fixed and readily specified set of defining features are called
   a.   This answer is incorrect because expected utilities are not relevant to this question. Review page 250 in your textbook.
   b.   This answer is incorrect because availability heuristics are relevant to a question on attribution. Review page 250 in your textbook.
   c.   For more information, see page 250 in your textbook.
   d.   This answer is incorrect because logical concepts have a clearly defined set of rules or properties. Review page 250 in your textbook.

7.2   Cognitive frameworks that represent our knowledge of and assumptions about the world are called
   a.   This answer is incorrect because visual images are limited to visual processes, not cognitive frameworks. Review page 251 in your textbook.
   b.   This answer is incorrect because these memories are for processing base information not frameworks. Review page 251 in your textbook.
   c.   For more information, see page 251 in your textbook.
   d.   This answer is incorrect because concepts are defined as mental categories for objects, events, etc. that represent our worlds. Review page 251 in your textbook.

7.3   Our tendency to gather evidence that will confirm rather than refute a hypothesis we believe is called
   a.   This answer is incorrect because functional bias implies that a bias is adaptable for an individual. Review page 255 in your textbook.
   b.   For more information, see page 255 in your textbook.
   c.   This answer is incorrect because oversight bias implies that a person has a bias concerning those things over which he or she has the responsibility to oversee. Review page 255 in your textbook.
   d.   This answer is incorrect because artificial intelligence involves the operating style of computers. Review page 255 in your textbook.

7.4   The _____ involves the tendency to judge events as more predictable after they occur than before they occur.
   a.   This answer is incorrect because this heuristic involves recalling an item that represents a category of interest. Review page 256 in your textbook.
   b.   This answer is incorrect because this bias involves selecting information that agrees with a previously held bias. Review page 256 in your textbook.
   c.   This answer is incorrect because this heuristic involves recalling information that is readily available cognitively. Review page 256 in your textbook.
   d.   For more information, see page 256 in your textbook.

7.5   Individuals sometimes take cognitive shortcuts, known as _____. in making decisions.
   a.   This answer is incorrect because syllogisms involve decision making using two alternatives. Review page 259 in your textbook.
   b.   For more information, see page 259 in your textbook.
   c.   This answer is incorrect because biases involve distorted perceptions that influence decision making. Review page 259 in your textbook.
   d.   This answer is incorrect because enhancements involve the addition of information to a question or problem. Review page 259 in your textbook.

7.6   According to the availability heuristic, the more easily we think of something, the more
   a.   For more information, see page 259 in your textbook.
   b.   This answer is incorrect because like or dislike is not part of this heuristic. Review page 259 in your textbook.
   c.   This answer is incorrect because like or dislike is not part of this heuristic. Review page 259 in your textbook.
   d.   This answer is incorrect because understanding is not a part of this heuristic. Review page 259 in your textbook.

7.7   When alternatives are presented in terms of the losses that might result, most people are
- a. This answer is incorrect because risk neutral is not relevant to this question. Review page 261 in your textbook.
- b. This answer is incorrect because risk considerate implies that we will consider risk, but does not specify under which circumstances will risk be considered. Review page 261 in your textbook.
- c. This answer is incorrect because risk averse occurs when potential gains are emphasized. Review page 261 in your textbook.
- d. For more information, see page 261 in your textbook.

7.8   Lisa is using the process of _____ when she goes toward the interstate highway when she is trying to find a restaurant in an unfamiliar town.
- a. This answer is incorrect because trial and error would involve just driving around the town hoping to find a restaurant. Review page 269 in your textbook.
- b. This answer is incorrect because an algorithm would involve driving down east and west streets (or north and south streets) because restaurants do have addresses. Review page 269 in your textbook.
- c. For more information, see page 269 in your textbook.
- d. This answer is incorrect because this analysis would involve determining the process to get to a specific end of a problem. Review page 269 in your textbook.

7.9   If an individual is asked to talk aloud while solving a problem, the experimenter is using
- a. This answer is incorrect because such processing implies developing a procedure for using language. Review page 270 in your textbook.
- b. For more information, see page 270 in your textbook.
- c. This answer is incorrect because such processing implies analyzing the structure of language. Review page 270 in your textbook.
- d. This answer is incorrect because such processing implies the use of language relative to the environment in which one lives. Review page 270 in your textbook.

7.10   A strong tendency to think of using objects only in ways they have been used before is called
- a. This answer is incorrect because entrapment involves capturing something of interest. Review page 271 in your textbook.
- b. This answer is incorrect because this process means continuing to commit to a course of action even in the face of evidence that success will not follow. Review page 271 in your textbook.
- c. This answer is incorrect because this bias means selecting information that agrees with previously held conclusions. Review page 271 in your textbook.
- d. For more information, see page 271 in your textbook.

7.11   A child is learning to understand meaning of words, which indicates the mechanism of
- a. For more information, see page 277 in your textbook.
- b. This answer is incorrect because this type of development involves being able to pronounce sounds and words of at least one language. Review page 277 in your textbook.
- c. This answer is incorrect because this type of development involves understanding the rules of a language. Review page 277 in your textbook.
- d. This answer is incorrect because this type of development involves understanding the arrangement of words into sentences. Review page 277 in your textbook.

7.12   Young children use single word utterances that convey much meaning. These utterances are
- a. This answer is incorrect because morphemes involve the smallest meaningful unit to make up a language. Review page 277 in your textbook.
- b. This answer is incorrect because phonemes involve speech sounds that make up a language. Review page 277 in your textbook.
- c. For more information, see page 277 in your textbook.
- d. This answer is incorrect because syntax involves the grammatical arrangement of words in a sentence. Review page 277 in your textbook.

7.13 The view that language shapes thought is the
   a. This answer is incorrect because this theory does not exist. Review page 278 in your textbook.
   b. For more information, see page 278 in your textbook.
   c. This answer is incorrect because this theory involves how individuals acquire behavior through social processes. Review page 278 in your textbook.
   d. This answer is incorrect because this hypothesis implies that there are innate mechanisms that influence our behavior. Review page 278 in your textbook.

7.14 Washoe, a female chimp, was taught to use and understand almost 200 words in
   a. This answer is incorrect because there is no such language system. Review page 279 in your textbook.
   b. This answer is incorrect because there is no such language system. Review page 279 in your textbook.
   c. This answer is incorrect because there is no such language system. Review page 279 in your textbook.
   d. For more information, see page 279 in your textbook.

7.15 Which of the following was **not** mentioned as a guideline for increasing the chances that decisions will be good ones?
   a. This answer is incorrect because this guideline was mentioned. Review page 281 in your textbook.
   b. This answer is incorrect because this guideline was mentioned. Review page 281 in your textbook.
   c. This answer is incorrect because this guideline was mentioned. Review page 281 in your textbook.
   d. For more information, see page 281 in your textbook.

7.16 The term _____ usually includes the mental activities associated with thought, decision making, language, and other higher mental processes.
   a. This answer is incorrect because introspection is a limited process of "seeing within." Review page 249 in your textbook.
   b. This answer is incorrect because reasoning is a process involving a limited number of variables. Review page 249 in your textbook.
   c. This answer is incorrect because thinking is subsumed in the items listed in the question. Review page 249 in your textbook.
   d. For more information, see page 249 in your textbook.

7.17 Which of the following may contain many different concepts?
   a. This answer is incorrect because phonemes are limited to language structure. Review page 251 in your textbook.
   b. For more information, see page 251 in your textbook.
   c. This answer is incorrect because morphemes are limited to language structure. Review page 251 in your textbook.
   d. This answer is incorrect because prototypes is the best example of something and may not involve concepts. Review page 251 in your textbook.

7.18 Cognitive activity that transforms information in order to reach specific conclusions is called
   a. This answer is incorrect because semantic development has to do with language. Review page 254 in your textbook.
   b. For more information, see page 254 in your textbook.
   c. This answer is incorrect because artificial intelligence is related to computers and their operation. Review page 254 in your textbook.
   d. This answer is incorrect because syntax is related to language structure. Review page 254 in your textbook.

7.19 The process of choosing among various courses of action or alternatives is
    a.   For more information, see page 258 in your textbook.
    b.   This answer is incorrect because escalation of commitment involves continuing to work on something when there is no chance of a favorable outcome. Review page 258 in your textbook.
    c.   This answer is incorrect because confirmation bias involves paying attention to information that confirms already held opinions. Review page 258 in your textbook.
    d.   This answer is incorrect because hindsight effect involves what might have been and the explanation for an event. Review page 258 in your textbook.

7.20 After watching television shows of crime in a large U. S. city, many individuals overestimate the likelihood of becoming a crime victim. This can be explained on the basis of
    a.   This answer is incorrect because hindsight effect involves what might have been and the explanation of an event. Review page 259 in your textbook.
    b.   For more information, see page 259 in your textbook.
    c.   This answer is incorrect because confirmation bias involves paying attention to information that confirms already held opinions. Review page 259 in your textbook.
    d.   This answer is incorrect because the representative heuristic is a way of explaining behavior based upon paying attention to characteristics that represent a category. Review page 259 in your textbook.

7.21 The tendency to become trapped in bad decisions is known as
    a.   This answer is incorrect because framing involves modifying the perception of an event. Review page 262 in your textbook.
    b.   This answer is incorrect because confirmation bias involves paying attention to information that confirms already held opinions. Review page 262 in your textbook.
    c.   This answer is incorrect because overconfidence does not imply that a person would continue in a bad decision. Review page 262 in your textbook.
    d.   For more information, see page 262 in your textbook.

7.22 The tendency to stick with a familiar method of solving particular types of problems is called
    a.   This answer is incorrect because functional fixedness relates to using tools only in the way they were designed. Review page 271 in your textbook.
    b.   This answer is incorrect because availability heuristic would involve remembering what was the most readily available information, whether familiar or not. Review page 271 in your textbook.
    c.   For more information, see page 271 in your textbook.
    d.   This answer is incorrect because cognitive dissonance is an attitude change technique. Review page 271 in your textbook.

7.23 The study of how computers perform actions that in humans require cognitive abilities is called
    a.   This answer is incorrect because computer psychology is not an area of psychology. Review page 272 in your textbook.
    b.   This answer is incorrect because electronic cognition is not a phenomenon. Review page 272 in your textbook.
    c.   For more information, see page 272 in your textbook.
    d.   This answer is incorrect because mechanical thought is not applicable to this question. Review page 272 in your textbook.

7.24 A system of symbols, plus rules for combining them, used to communicate information is called
    a.   This answer is incorrect because intelligence is not directly related to communication of symbols. Review page 275 in your textbook.
    b.   For more information, see page 275 in your textbook.
    c.   This answer is incorrect because thinking, while involving symbols, may not be related to communication. Review page 275 in your textbook.
    d.   This answer is incorrect because reasoning is not necessarily related to communication. Review page 275 in your textbook.

7.25 Language seems to be learned much more easily during early childhood than at any other time of life, a finding that is termed a(n)

a. This answer is incorrect because operating principles are applicable to all ages. Review page 276 in your textbook.

b. This answer is incorrect because linguistic phase is not really a phenomenon. Review page 276 in your textbook.

c. For more information, see page 276 in your textbook.

d. This answer is incorrect because phonological loop involves the structure of language not time for learning a language. Review page 276 in your textbook.

Chapter 7 - Practice Test Answers

Question	Answer
7.1	c
7.2	c
7.3	b
7.4	d
7.5	b
7.6	a
7.7	d
7.8	c
7.9	b
7.10	d
7.11	a
7.12	c
7.13	b
7.14	d
7.15	d
7.16	d
7.17	b
7.18	b
7.19	a
7.20	b
7.21	d
7.22	c
7.23	c
7.24	b
7.25	c

Chapter 8 - Practice Test

8.1   Recent evidence indicates that infants only a few months old spent more time looking:
   a.   in the direction of the sound of familiar sounds.
   b.   in the direction of the sound of another baby's name.
   c.   in the direction of the sound of their own names.
   d.   in the direction of the sound of consistent-stress names.

8.2   Research by Frantz and others on the visual preferences of infants showed that they prefer to look at
   a.   sharp angles.
   b.   human faces.
   c.   bright colors.
   d.   funny pictures.

8.3   The major disadvantage of cross-sectional research is that
   a.   differences between groups may be due to different experiences not related to age.
   b.   it is often difficult to contact the same individuals over and over again for a long time.
   c.   sometimes the type of groups needed for this research is difficult to identify.
   d.   it is more time-consuming and expensive to conduct than other types of research.

8.4   A theory that proposes that all human beings go through an orderly and predictable series of changes is known as
   a.   a synchronous theory.
   b.   a successive theory.
   c.   an asynchronous theory.
   d.   a stage theory

8.5   In Piaget's theory of cognitive development, children in the sensorimotor stage
   a.   know the world only through muscle activities and sensory impressions.
   b.   are struggling with the basic concepts of logic and conservation.
   c.   are focused inward on their growing mental abilities, not on their environment.
   d.   are particularly in need of warm, loving support from their parents.

8.6   During Piaget's formal operations period, individuals are said to become capable of
   a.   reversibility.
   b.   hypothetico-deductive reasoning.
   c.   conservation.
   d.   egocentrism

8.7   Knowledge pertaining to specific areas of life and activity is called
   a.   maintenance knowledge.
   b.   factual information.
   c.   context-dependent memory.
   d.   domain-specific knowledge.

8.8   When we become aware of our own cognitive processes, we are involved in
   a.   hypercognition.
   b.   metacognition.
   c.   schematic processing
   d.   cognitive enhancement.

8.9 Older children, compared to younger children, are better able to use the process of _____, a process by which new information is linked to existing knowledge.
   a. constructivism
   b. scaffolding
   c. elaboration
   d. rehearsal

8.10 Ralph believes that moral decisions should be based upon the rule of law in a society, therefore he is at the _____ level of moral development.
   a. preconventional
   b. pseudoconventional
   c. conventional
   d. postconventional

8.11 Early research on how Kohlberg's theory of moral development applies to males and females indicated that
   a. females progress to higher stages than males do.
   b. males progress to higher stages than females do.
   c. males and females progress through the stages equally.
   d. the theory has never been tested with females.

8.12 A child who falls and then looks at his father to see whether he should cry or not is using
   a. nonverbal communication.
   b. paternal reaction.
   c. parental communication.
   d. social referencing.

8.13 Research indicates that there are differences in children's _____, in that some children are easy, some are difficult, and some are slow-to-warm-up.
   a. cognitions
   b. abilities.
   c. temperament.
   d. communication.

8.14 When studying attachment, research results indicate that the vast majority of American middle-class infants show
   a. secure attachment.
   b. avoidant attachment.
   c. ambivalent attachment.
   d. disoriented attachment.

8.15 Harlow's research with monkeys showed that
   a. baby monkeys' attachments to their cloth mother could be reversed by rejection.
   b. the satisfaction provided by feeding is sufficient for attachment.
   c. the satisfaction provided by feeding is not sufficient for attachment.
   d. attachment in human infants is not the same as attachment in monkeys.

8.16 Changes that are determined largely by our genes are known as
   a. assimilation.
   b. instability.
   c. maturation.
   d. accommodation.

8.17 Infants only two hours can be classically conditioned, but primarily with stimuli that have _____ for babies.
a. survival value
b. aversive consequences
c. limited application
d. social implications

8.18 Which of the following techniques is most likely to be affected by subject attrition and practice effects?
a. cross-sectional method
b. longitudinal method
c. hypothetical-deductive method
d. meta-analysis

8.19 According to Piaget, the process of building mental representations of the world through direct interaction with it is
a. constructivism.
b. egocentrism.
c. metacognition.
d. conservation.

8.20 The lack of serialization and the lack of principles of conservation accompanied with egocentric thought are characteristic of Piaget's
a. formal operations stage.
b. preoperational stage.
c. concrete operations stage.
d. object permanence stage.

8.21 Older children, compared to younger children, are better able to use the process of _____, a process by which new information is linked to existing knowledge.
a. constructivism
b. scaffolding
c. elaboration
d. rehearsal

8.22 At the _____ level of moral development, we tend to judge morality in terms of what supports and preserves the social order.
a. preconventional
b. conventional
c. postconventional
d. abstract

8.23 Infant emotional development is measured by
a. facial expressions.
b. EEG recordings.
c. body gestures.
d. neurological calculations.

8.24 Our ability to recognize the emotions of others, to understand these emotions, and to a degree, experience them ourselves is known as
a. care-giving.
b. empathy.
c. compassion.
d. emotionality.

8.25   Relationships involving strong mutual affectional ties between two persons are called
    a.   attachments.
    b.   friendships.
    c.   families.
    d.   competitors.

Chapter 8 - Practice Test Answer Justifications

8.1   Recent evidence indicates that infants only a few months old spent more time looking
    a.   This answer is incorrect because infants usually attend to unfamiliar sounds rather than sounds with which they have become familiar. Review page 295 in your textbook.
    b.   This answer is incorrect because infants usually are especially attentive to the sound of their own names. Review page 295 in your textbook.
    c.   For more information, see page 295 in your textbook.
    d.   This answer is incorrect because infants usually attend to the sound of changing patterns of stress, such as <u>mama</u> rather than mama. Review page 295 in your textbook.

8.2   Research by Frantz and others on the visual preferences of infants showed that they prefer to look at
    a.   This answer is incorrect because even though infants preferred patterns over plain targets, they most preferred human faces. Review page 295 in your textbook.
    b.   For more information, see page 295 in your textbook.
    c.   This answer is incorrect because even though infants preferred bright colors over dull colors, they most preferred human faces. Review page 295 in your textbook.
    d.   This answer is incorrect because infants would have difficulty defining what is funny. Review page 295 in your textbook.

8.3   The major disadvantage of cross-sectional research is that
    a.   For more information, see page 297 in your textbook.
    b.   This answer is incorrect because it is describing longitudinal research. Review page 297 in your textbook.
    c.   This answer is incorrect because the group is defined in terms of a specific variable, usually age. Review page 297 in your textbook.
    d.   This answer is incorrect because this type of research is usually fairly quick and inexpensive to conduct in comparison to other methods. Review page 297 in your textbook.

8.4   A theory that proposes that all human beings go through an orderly and predictable series of changes is known as
    a.   This answer is incorrect because a synchronous theory would imply that development occurred at the same time or were in concert with one another. Review page 298 in your textbook.
    b.   This answer is incorrect because a successive theory would imply that development occurred in a continuous sequence with no plateaus. Review page 298 in your textbook.
    c.   This answer is incorrect because an asynchronous theory would imply that there was no coordination regarding the development. Review page 298 in your textbook.
    d.   For more information, see page 298 in your textbook.

8.5   In Piaget's theory of cognitive development, children in the sensorimotor stage
    a.   For more information, see page 299 in your textbook.
    b.   This answer is incorrect because these concepts are much too complicated for children at this age (18-24 months). Review page 299 in your textbook.
    c.   This answer is incorrect because infants at this age (18-24 months) are not able to comprehend their own abilities. Review page 299 in your textbook.
    d.   This answer is incorrect because children need this type of support at all levels. Review page 299 in your textbook.

8.6   During Piaget's formal operations period, individuals are said to become capable of
    a.   This answer is incorrect because individuals already have this ability by the time they reach the formal operations period. Review page 301 in your textbook.
    b.   For more information, see page 301 in your textbook.
    c.   This answer is incorrect because individuals already have this ability by the time they reach the formal operations period. Review page 301 in your textbook.
    d.   This answer is incorrect because individuals already have this ability by the time they reach the formal operations period. Review page 301 in your textbook.

8.7   Knowledge pertaining to specific areas of life and activity is called
   a.   This answer is incorrect because such knowledge may go across several areas of life. Review page 304 in your textbook.
   b.   This answer is incorrect because such information may apply to several areas of life. Review page 304 in your textbook.
   c.   This answer is incorrect because such memory implies that recall will be affected by the situation in which we learned material. Review page 304 in your textbook.
   d.   For more information, see page 304 in your textbook.

8.8   When we become aware of our own cognitive processes, we are involved in
   a.   This answer is incorrect because hypercognition implies a super level of cognition, not awareness of our own cognitive processes. Review page 307 in your textbook.
   b.   For more information, see page 307 in your textbook.
   c.   This answer is incorrect because schematic processing involves a way in which we process information, not the awareness of how we process information. Review page 307 in your textbook.
   d.   This answer is incorrect because such enhancement would involve making our cognition better, not how we think about our cognition. Review page 307 in your textbook.

8.9   Older children, compared to younger children, are better able to use the process of _____, a process by which new information is linked to existing knowledge.
   a.   This answer is incorrect because constructivism involves building a knowledge of the world by interacting with it. Review page 307 in your textbook.
   b.   This answer is incorrect because scaffolding involves adults giving children mental structures to use as they master new tasks and ways of thinking. Review page 307 in your textbook.
   c.   For more information, see page 307 in your textbook.
   d.   This answer is incorrect because rehearsal involves repetition of information. Review page 307 in your textbook.

8.10   Ralph believes that moral decisions should be based upon the rule of law in a society, therefore he is at the _____ level of moral development.
   a.   This answer is incorrect because preconventional involves judging morality in terms of consequences. Review page 308 in your textbook.
   b.   This answer is incorrect because there is no pseudoconventional level in Kohlberg's theory. Review page 308 in your textbook.
   c.   For more information, see page 308 in your textbook.
   d.   This answer is incorrect because postconventional involves judging morality in terms of abstract principles and values. Review page 308 in your textbook.

8.11   Early research on how Kohlberg's theory of moral development applies to males and females indicated that
   a.   For more information, see page 310 in your textbook.
   b.   This answer is incorrect because the research found that females progressed to higher levels. Review page 310 in your textbook.
   c.   This answer is incorrect because individuals tend to progress through the stages quite inconsistently, regardless of gender. Review page 310 in your textbook.
   d.   This answer is incorrect because the theory was tested with females. Review page 310 in your textbook.

8.12   A child who falls and then looks at his father to see whether he should cry or not is using
   a.   This answer is incorrect because he is not communicating with his father in a nonverbal way. Review page 311 in your textbook.
   b.   This answer is incorrect because paternal reaction would be the reaction of the parent. Review page 311 in your textbook.
   c.   This answer is incorrect because such communication would be on the part of the parent. Review page 311 in your textbook.
   d.   For more information, see page 311 in your textbook.

8.13 Research indicates that there are differences in children's _____, in that some children are easy, some are difficult, and some are slow-to-warm-up.
  a. This answer is incorrect because cognitions do not involve the described activities. Review page 312 in your textbook.
  b. This answer is incorrect because abilities do not involve the described activities. Review page 312 in your textbook.
  c. For more information, see page 312 in your textbook.
  d. This answer is incorrect because communication does not involve the described activities. Review page 312 in your textbook.

8.14 When studying attachment, research results indicate that the vast majority of American middle-class infants show
  a. For more information, see page 314 in your textbook.
  b. This answer is incorrect because this type of attachment is most often shown by German infants. Review page 314 in your textbook.
  c. This answer is incorrect because there is speculation if this type of attachment exists. Review page 314 in your textbook.
  d. This answer is incorrect because most infants do not show this type of attachment. Review page 314 in your textbook.

8.15 Harlow's research with monkeys indicated that
  a. This answer is incorrect because the monkeys would simply wait for the rejection period to cease and then go back to the cloth mother. Review page 317 in your textbook.
  b. This answer is incorrect because the monkeys needed contact comfort. Review page 317 in your textbook.
  c. For more information, see page 317 in your textbook.
  d. This answer is incorrect because Harlow's research dealt with monkeys and attachment in humans was irrelevant to his findings. Review page 317 in your textbook.

8.16 Changes that are determined largely by our genes are known as
  a. This answer is incorrect because assimilation is a cognitive activity. Review page 286 in your textbook.
  b. This answer is incorrect because instability is one of the major issues of psychology. Review page 286 in your textbook.
  c. For more information, see page 286 in your textbook.
  d. This answer is incorrect because accommodation is a cognitive activity.

8.17 Infants only two hours old can be classically conditioned, but primarily with stimuli that have _____ for babies.
  a. For more information, see page 294 in your textbook.
  b. This answer is incorrect because conditioning involving aversive consequences could lead to damage to a infant that young. Review page 294 in your textbook.
  c. This answer is incorrect because limited application would be applicable to almost all stimuli presented to babies this young. Review page 294 in your textbook.
  d. This answer is incorrect because social implications are not a major relevant issue for babies this young. Review page 294 in your textbook.

8.18   Which of the following techniques is most likely to be affected by subject attrition and
        practice effects?
        a.   This answer is incorrect because the cross-sectional method does not involve additional contact with
              participants.
        b.   For more information, see page 297 in your textbook.
        c.   This answer is incorrect because the hypothetical-deductive method is not really a developmental
              technique, but more of a method of generating theoretical questions. Review page 297 in your
              textbook.
        d.   This answer is incorrect because meta-analysis does not involve participants. Review page 297 in
              your textbook.

8.19   According to Piaget, the process of building mental representations of the world through direct
        interaction with it is
        a.   For more information, see page 299 in your textbook.
        b.   This answer is incorrect because egocentrism involves a distorted personal view of the world. Review
              page 299 in your textbook.
        c.   This answer is incorrect because metacognition involves a person's "theory of mind." Review299 page
              in your textbook.
        d.   This answer is incorrect because the principle of conservation means that a person realizes that
              volume, amount, etc. are the same regardless of shape, form, etc. Review page 299 in your textbook..

8.20   The lack of serialization and the lack of principles of conservation accompanied with egocentric
        thought are characteristic of Piaget's
        a.   This answer is incorrect because the formal operations stage would include these operations. Review
              page 301 in your textbook.
        b.   For more information, see page 301 in your textbook.
        c.   This answer is incorrect because the concrete operations stage would include these operations. Review
              page 301 in your textbook.
        d.   This answer is incorrect because there is no formal object permanence stage. Review page 301 in your
              textbook.

8.21   Older children, compared to younger children, are better able to use the process of _____, a process by
        which new information is linked to existing knowledge.
        a.   This answer is incorrect because the processes of constructivism are relevant to all ages. Review page
              307 in your textbook.
        b.   This answer is incorrect because the principle of scaffolding is a social process in which children
              master new tasks using mental structures provided by adults. Review page 307 in your textbook.
        c.   For more information, see page 307 in your textbook.
        d.   This answer is incorrect because rehearsal is a process repetition, not linkage. Review page 307 in
              your textbook.

8.22   At the _____ level of moral development, we tend to judge morality in terms of what supports
        and preserves the social order.
        a.   This answer is incorrect because the preconventional level involves consequences of actions. Review
              page 308 in your textbook.
        b.   For more information, see page 308 in your textbook.
        c.   This answer is incorrect because the postconventional level involves abstract principles. Review page
              308 in your textbook.
        d.   This answer is incorrect because abstract is not relevant to this question. Review page 308 in your
              textbook.

8.23 Infant emotional development is measured by
   a. For more information, see page 311 in your textbook.
   b. This answer is incorrect because EEG recordings would not give information about emotions. Review page 311 in your textbook.
   c. This answer is incorrect because body gestures would not give information about development and would also involve social factors. Review page 311 in your textbook.
   d. This answer is incorrect because neurological calculations would not give information about emotional development. Review page 311 in your textbook.

8.24 Our ability to recognize the emotions of others, to understand these emotions, and to a degree, experience them ourselves is known as
   a. This answer is incorrect because care-giving is related to providing service when needed. Review page 313 in your textbook.
   b. For more information, see page 313 in your textbook.
   c. This answer is incorrect because compassion is a feeling that does not necessarily involve being intimate with the emotions of others. Review page 313 in your textbook.
   d. This answer is incorrect because emotionality is a trait, but not necessarily involving other individuals. Review page 313 in your textbook.

8.25 Relationships involving strong mutual affectional ties between two persons are called
   a. This answer is incorrect because attachments may be one-sided. Review page 317 in your textbook.
   b. For more information, see page 317 in your textbook.
   c. This answer is incorrect because families may involve more than two people. Review page 317 in your textbook.
   d. This answer is incorrect because competitors may not involve an affective relationship. Review page 317 in your textbook.

Chapter 8 - Practice Test Answers

Question	Answer
8.1	c
8.2	b
8.3	a
8.4	d
8.5	a
8.6	b
8.7	d
8.8	b
8.9	c
8.10	c
8.11	a
8.12	d
8.13	c
8.14	a
8.15	c
8.16	c
8.17	a
8.18	b
8.19	a
8.20	b
8.21	c
8.22	b
8.23	a
8.24	b
8.25	b

Chapter 9 - Practice Test

9.1   Adolescence is traditionally viewed as beginning with the
    a.   onset of puberty.
    b.   ending of puberty.
    c.   entrance into high school.
    d.   establishment of gender identity.

9.2   The belief that knowledge is a property of the real world and that there are definite facts that be acquired is known as
    a.   a realist approach to knowledge.
    b.   a relativist approach to knowledge.
    c.   a defended realism approach.
    d.   a dogmatism-skepticism approach.

9.3   Erikson is to Piaget as
    a.   cognitive development is to stage theory.
    b.   social development is to cognitive development.
    c.   intelligence is to emotional development.
    d.   continuity is to education.

9.4   By asking questions such as, "Who am I?" "What am I going to become?", Ralph is in which stage of Erickson's theory?
    a.   integrity vs. despair
    b.   intimacy vs. isolation
    c.   autonomy vs. shame and doubt
    d.   identity vs. role confusion

9.5   A _____ is a family that does not meet the needs of children.
    a.   reckless family
    b.   negative family
    c.   dysfunctional family.
    d.   developmental family

9.6   Two major approaches to adult development include
    a.   stage theory approach and contextual approach.
    b.   fluid approach and crystallized approach.
    c.   dysfunctional approach and autonomy approach.
    d.   transitional approach and maturation approach.

9.7   Which of the following is most likely to be the best predictor of physical vigor and health as we age?
    a.   biological age
    b.   life-style
    c.   family history
    d.   career

9.8   With respect to short-term memory, older persons in comparison to young adults have a
    a.   slightly greater capacity.
    b.   slightly smaller capacity.
    c.   similar capacity.
    d.   extremely smaller capacity.

9.9 Research suggesting that intelligence declines with age was based on the _____ research model.
   a. cross-sectional
   b. longitudinal
   c. longitudinal-sequential
   d. experimental

9.10 Research indicates that _____ increases into the early twenties, and then gradually declines.
   a. crystallized intelligence
   b. general intelligence
   c. procedural intelligence
   d. fluid intelligence

9.11 In Levinson's theory concerning adult development, the underlying pattern or design of a person's life is called
   a. life structure.
   b. structural integrity.
   c. sequential development.
   d. transitional structure.

9.12 When individuals have to deal with the possibility of upcoming retirement, they are in the
   a. retirement transition.
   b. midlife transition.
   c. late-adult transition.
   d. elderly transition.

9.13 Levinson's theory is a _____ in that it suggests that all people pass through a series of eras and transitions.
   a. continuous theory
   b. direction theory
   c. transition theory
   d. stage theory

9.14 Physiological death refers to a time when
   a. there is no electrical activity in the brain for ten minutes.
   b. all biological activities that sustain life has stopped.
   c. there is no electrical activity in the cerebral cortex.
   d. people give up their relationships with the dead one.

9.15 Bereavement refers to processes involved in
   a. coming to terms with one's imminent death.
   b. recovering from a violent assault.
   c. dealing with the death of a loved one.
   d. the physical changes of adulthood.

9.16 A sudden spurt in physical growth accompanied by sexual maturity defines
   a. gender identity.
   b. puberty.
   c. adolescence.
   d. androgyny.

9.17 The extent to which parents are strict or controlling and confront their children when they do not meet parental expectations is called
   a. parental responsiveness.
   b. parental demandingness.
   c. parental confrontation.
   d. parental involvement.

9.18   Erikson's fifth stage occurs during adolescence where adolescents seek to establish an
        understanding of their own unique traits and what is really of central importance to them.
        This stage centers around
        a.   trust versus mistrust.
        b.   initiative versus guilt.
        c.   identity versus role confusion.
        d.   autonomy versus shame and doubt.

9.19   A theory of adult development that emphasizes the resolution of internal conflicts that
        must be faced at each stage is called a(n) _____ theory.
        a.   generative
        b.   elaborative
        c.   life-event
        d.   crisis

9.20   The ecological systems theory postulates four levels of systems in which individuals and their ecology
        interact. Which of the following is **not** one of the four ecological systems?
        a.   macrosystem
        b.   mesosystem
        c.   ecosystem
        d.   microsystem

9.21   The concept of _____ is based upon the idea that changes in a person's body is caused by the passage
        of time and perhaps by genetic factors.
        a.   secondary aging
        b.   primary aging
        c.   tertiary aging
        d.   biological aging

9.22   Research indicates that _____ increases into the early twenties, and then gradually declines.
        a.   crystallized intelligence
        b.   general intelligence
        c.   procedural intelligence
        d.   fluid intelligence

9.23   In Levinson's theory of adult development, a _____ is an older and more experienced individual
        who helps guide a younger person.
        a.   father-figure
        b.   proprietor
        c.   mentor
        d.   counselor

9.24   The personality trait of _____ seems to be a significant predictor of long life.
        a.   conscientiousness
        b.   compulsiveness
        c.   gregariousness
        d.   sociability

9.25   According to Kubler-Ross, the first stage of the dying process is
        a.   denial.
        b.   anger.
        c.   depression.
        d.   bargaining.

Chapter 9 - Practice Test Answer Justifications

9.1   Adolescence is traditionally viewed as beginning with the
        a.   For more information, see page 330 in your textbook.
        b.   This answer is incorrect because the ending of puberty occurs during adolescence. Review page 330 in your textbook.
        c.   This answer is incorrect because grade in school is not a part of human development. Review page 330 in your textbook.
        d.   This answer is incorrect because gender identity is established during childhood. Review page 330 in your textbook.

9.2   The belief that knowledge is a property of the real world and that there are definite facts that be acquired is known as
        a.   For more information, see page 332 in your textbook.
        b.   This answer is incorrect because a relativist approach would recognize that there are different interpretations of the same information by different people. Review page 332 in your textbook.
        c.   This answer is incorrect because a defended realism approach recognizes the difference between facts and opinions. Review page 332 in your textbook.
        d.   This answer is incorrect because a dogmatism-skepticism approach is the alternation between blind faith in authority and doubting everything. Review page 332 in your textbook.

9.3   Erikson is to Piaget as
        a.   This answer is incorrect because Erikson's theory is not associated with cognitive development. Review page 335 in your textbook.
        b.   For more information, see page 335 in your textbook.
        c.   This answer is incorrect because Erikson's theory is not associated with intelligence. Review page 335 in your textbook.
        d.   This answer is incorrect because these two concepts are not directly associated with the two individuals. Review page 335 in your textbook.

9.4   By asking questions such as, "Who am I?" "What am I going to become?", Ralph is in which stage of Erickson's theory?
        a.   This answer is incorrect because this crisis occurs at the end of someone's life at which time that person is evaluating his or her life. Review page 336 in your textbook.
        b.   This answer is incorrect because this crisis involves the development of intimate relationships. Review page 336 in your textbook.
        c.   This answer is incorrect because this crisis occurs during the second year of life and a child would not have the cognitive ability to consider issues such as those in the questions. Review page 336 in your textbook.
        d.   For more information, see page 336 in your textbook.

9.5   A _____ is a family that does not meet the needs of children.
        a.   This answer is incorrect because such a family has not been clearly identified. Review page 341 in your textbook.
        b.   This answer is incorrect because such a family may meet the needs of children, just not in a positive way. Review page 341 in your textbook.
        c.   For more information, see page 341 in your textbook.
        d.   This answer is incorrect because all families are developmental in some way or another. Review page 341 your textbook.

9.6   Two major approaches to adult development include
        a. For more information, see page 344 in your textbook.
        b. This answer is incorrect because such approaches are not applicable to adult development. Review page 344 in your textbook.
        c. This answer is incorrect because such approaches are not applicable to adult development. Review page 344 in your textbook.
        d. This answer is incorrect because such approaches are not applicable to adult development. Review page 344 in your textbook.

9.7   Which of the following is most likely to be the best predictor of physical vigor and health as we age?
        a. This answer is incorrect because the impact of biological age can be influenced by environmental factors. Review page 349 in your textbook.
        b. For more information, see page 349 in your textbook.
        c. This answer is incorrect because even though family history is important, its influence can be mediated by environmental factors. Review page 349 in your textbook.
        d. This answer is incorrect because the influence of a career can be mediated by environmental factors. Review page 349 in your textbook.

9.8   With respect to short-term memory, older persons in comparison to young adults have a(n)
        a. This answer is incorrect because the capacity is essentially the same. Review page 351 in your textbook.
        b. This answer is incorrect because the capacity is essentially the same. Review page 351 in your textbook.
        c. For more information, see page 351 in your textbook.
        d. This answer is incorrect because the capacity is essentially the same. Review page 351 in your textbook.

9.9   Research suggesting that intelligence declines with age was based on the _____ research model.
        a. For more information, see page 352 in your textbook.
        b. This answer is incorrect because this research method yields different results. Review page 352 in your textbook.
        c. This answer is incorrect because this method is not used. Review page 352 in your textbook.
        d. This answer is incorrect because the experimental method is the general technique, and not a specific research model. Review page 352 in your textbook.

9.10   Research indicates that _____ increases into the early twenties, and then gradually declines.
        a. This answer is incorrect because this type of intelligence tends to increase over the life span. Review page 354 in your textbook.
        b. This answer is incorrect because general intelligence does not increase into the early twenties. Review page 354 in your textbook.
        c. This answer is incorrect because procedural intelligence does not increase into the early twenties. Review page 354 in your textbook.
        d. For more information, see page 354 in your textbook.

9.11   In Levinson's theory concerning adult development, the underlying pattern or design of a person's life is called
        a. For more information, see page 356 in your textbook.
        b. This answer is incorrect because structural integrity is not a part of Levinson's theory. Review page 356 in your textbook.
        c. This answer is incorrect because sequential development is not a part of Levinson's theory. Review page 356 in your textbook.
        d. This answer is incorrect because even though there are transitional periods in Levinson's theory, transitional structure is not a part of Levinson's theory. Review page 356 in your textbook.

9.12   When individuals have to deal with the possibility of upcoming retirement, they are in the
   a.   This answer is incorrect because there is no retirement transition stage in Levinson's theory. Review page 357 in your textbook.
   b.   This answer is incorrect because this transition occurs long before retirement is usually considered. Review page 357 in your textbook.
   c.   For more information, see page 357 in your textbook.
   d.   This answer is incorrect because there is no such transition in Levinson's theory. Review page 357 in your textbook.

9.13   Levinson's theory is a _____ in that it suggests that all people pass through a series of eras and transitions.
   a.   This answer is incorrect because such a theory would mean that development was a continuous process, not made up of plateaus of development. Review page 358 in your textbook.
   b.   This answer is incorrect because direction theory is not a category of theories. Review page 358 in your textbook.
   c.   This answer is incorrect because transition theory is not a category of theories. Review page 358 in your textbook.
   d.   For more information, see page 358 in your textbook.

9.14   Physiological death refers to a time when
   a.   This answer is incorrect because this is the definition of brain death. Review page 361 in your textbook.
   b.   For more information, see page 361 in your textbook.
   c.   This answer is incorrect because this is the definition of cerebral death. Review page 361 in your textbook.
   d.   This answer is incorrect because this is the definition of social death. Review page 361 in your textbook.

9.15   Bereavement refers to processes involved in
   a.   This answer is incorrect because bereavement involves the death of someone else. Review page 363 in your textbook.
   b.   This answer is incorrect because bereavement involves the death of someone else. Review page 363 in your textbook.
   c.   For more information, see page 363 in your textbook.
   d.   This answer is incorrect because bereavement involves the death of someone else. Review page 363 in your textbook.

9.16   A sudden spurt in physical growth accompanied by sexual maturity defines
   a.   This answer is incorrect because gender identity is not directly related to a growth spurt. Review page 331 in your textbook.
   b.   For more information, see page 331 in your textbook.
   c.   This answer is incorrect because adolescence is a social phenomenon, not a physical one. Review page 331 in your textbook.
   d.   This answer is incorrect because androgyny is related to the combination of female and male traits. Review page 331 in your textbook.

9.17   The extent to which parents are strict or controlling and confront their children when they do not meet parental expectations is called
   a.   This answer is incorrect because parental responsiveness involves how much parents provide care for their children. Review page 334 in your textbook.
   b.   For more information, see page 334 in your textbook.
   c.   This answer is incorrect because parental confrontation is a process, not a broad approach to child development. Review page 334 in your textbook.
   d.   This answer is incorrect because parental involvement is an activity, not a broad approach to child development. Review page 334 in your textbook.

9.18   Erikson's fifth stage occurs during adolescence where adolescents seek to establish an understanding of their own unique traits and what is really of central importance to them. This stage centers around
   a.   This answer is incorrect because trust versus mistrust is the first stage. Review page 336 in your textbook.
   b.   This answer is incorrect because initiative versus guilt is the third stage. Review page 336 in your textbook.
   c.   For more information, see page 336 in your textbook.
   d.   This answer is incorrect because autonomy versus shame and doubt is the second stage. Review page 336 in your textbook.

9.19   A theory of adult development that emphasizes the resolution of internal conflicts that must be faced at each stage is called a(n) _____ theory.
   a.   This answer is incorrect because a generative is not a type of developmental theory. Review page 344 in your textbook.
   b.   This answer is incorrect because an elaborative theory is not a type of developmental theory. Review page 344 in your textbook.
   c.   This answer is incorrect because a life-event theory is dependent upon situations in a person's life, not necessarily internal conflicts. Review page 344 in your textbook.
   d.   For more information, see page 344 in your textbook.

9.20   The ecological systems theory postulates four levels of systems in which individuals and their ecology interact. Which of the following is **not** one of the four ecological systems?
   a.   This answer is incorrect because macrosystem is one of the four ecological systems. Review page 345 in your textbook.
   b.   This answer is incorrect because mesosystem is one of the four ecological systems. Review page 345 in your textbook.
   c.   For more information, see page 345 in your textbook.
   d.   This answer is incorrect because microsystem is one of the four ecological systems. Review page 345 in your textbook.

9.21   The concept of _____ is based upon the idea that changes in a person's body is caused by the passage of time and perhaps by genetic factors.
   a.   For more information, see page 350 in your textbook.
   b.   This answer is incorrect because secondary aging has to do with lifestyle. Review page 350 in your textbook.
   c.   This answer is incorrect because tertiary aging is not a type of aging. Review page 350 in your textbook.
   d.   This answer is incorrect because biological aging may not include genetic factors. Review page 350 in your textbook.

9.22   Research indicates that _____ increases into the early twenties, and then gradually declines.
   a.   This answer is incorrect because crystallized intelligence tends to increase across the lifespan. Review page 354 in your textbook.
   b.   This answer is incorrect because general intelligence is similar to practical intelligence and tends to increase across the lifespan. Review page 354 in your textbook.
   c.   This answer is incorrect because procedural intelligence is not a specific type of intelligence. Review page 354 in your textbook.
   d.   For more information, see page 354 in your textbook.

9.23   In Levinson's theory of adult development, a _____ is an older and more experienced individual who helps guide a younger person.
   a.   This answer is incorrect because a father-figure implies emotional commitment. Review page 356 in your textbook.
   b.   This answer is incorrect because a proprietor is someone who owns a business. Review page 356 in your textbook.
   c.   For more information, see page 356 in your textbook.
   d.   This answer is incorrect because a counselor is involved in working out personal problems. Review page 356 in your textbook.

9.24   The personality trait of _____ seems to be a significant predictor of long life.
   a.   For more information, see page 361 in your textbook.
   b.   This answer is incorrect because compulsiveness could be so severe that it would be a limiting factor in living. Review page 361 in your textbook.
   c.   This answer is incorrect because gregariousness may increase the wear and tear on one's body. Review page 361 in your textbook.
   d.   This answer is incorrect because sociability involves getting along with others, but not necessarily taking care of one's own life. Review page 361 in your textbook.

9.25   According to Kubler-Ross, the first stage of the dying process is
   a.   For more information, see page 362 in your textbook.
   b.   This answer is incorrect because anger is the second stage. Review page 362 in your textbook.
   c.   This answer is incorrect because depression is the fourth stage. Review page 362 in your textbook.
   d.   This answer is incorrect because bargaining is the third stage. Review page 362 in your textbook.

Chapter 9 - Practice Test Answers

Question	Answer
9.1	a
9.2	a
9.3	b
9.4	d
9.5	c
9.6	a
9.7	b
9.8	c
9.9	a
9.10	d
9.11	a
9.12	c
9.13	d
9.14	b
9.15	c
9.16	b
9.17	b
9.18	c
9.19	d
9.20	c
9.21	a
9.22	d
9.23	c
9.24	a
9.25	a

Chapter 10 - Practice Test

10.1 Internal processes that activate, guide, and maintain behavior over time are called:
   a. reinforcement.
   b. motivation.
   c. instincts.
   d. emotions.

10.2 One major problem with drive theory of motivation is that
   a. humans will sometimes engage in behaviors that increase a drive.
   b. humans will sometimes engage in behaviors that decrease a drive.
   c. humans will sometimes engage in behaviors that are difficult to perform.
   d. humans will sometimes engage in behaviors that are easy to perform.

10.3 Arousal theories of motivation focus on an organism's efforts to
   a. maintain their basic biological systems so they can survive.
   b. reach a goal it believes to be reasonable and important.
   c. achieve an optimum level of nervous system activation.
   d. establish a sense of self-worth and personal growth.

10.4 One theory of motivation that involves an arrangement of needs from the most basic to the highest level is called
   a. configuration of needs.
   b. hierarchy of needs
   c. needs pyramid
   d. needs scale

10.5 The Pima of Arizona are a good example of the role of _____ in the determination of one's weight.
   a. environmental factors
   b. cognitive factors
   c. social factors
   d. genetic factors

10.6 In comparison to non-obese individuals, individuals who suffer from obesity seem to respond more strongly to
   a. reduced lipid levels.
   b. reduced glucose levels.
   c. external food cues.
   d. internal hunger pangs.

10.7 The desire to harm or injure someone else is called
   a. aggressive motivation.
   b. hurtful aggression.
   c. injurious aggression.
   d. aggression compulsion

10.8 Ralph experienced _____ when he was in a hurry to get to his job interview, but found that his route was blocked by a long line of rail cars.
   a. conflagration
   b. frustration
   c. aggression
   d. contagion

10.9   Violent outbursts in which employees attack and even kill employee colleagues are called:
   a.   workplace violence.
   b.   workplace provocation.
   c.   colleague violence.
   d.   employee violence.

10.10   Since Lisa is always trying to succeed in the tasks she undertakes, she would be classified as high in
   a.   achievement motivation.
   b.   affiliation motivation.
   c.   contagion motivation.
   d.   accomplishment motivation.

10.11   Ralph is high in _____ since he plays the piano because he likes to play the piano.
   a.   altruistic motivation
   b.   extrinsic motivation
   c.   musical motivation
   d.   intrinsic motivation

10.12   Lisa truly enjoys reading. If given money for reading at a certain rate, her reading performance will likely:
   a.   be unchanged.
   b.   be enhanced.
   c.   be reduced.
   d.   be selective.

10.13   Providing a ready excuse for potentially poor performance is called
   a.   lying.
   b.   deception.
   c.   self-handicapping.
   d.   self-serving.

10.14   It appears that the _____ seems to be specialized for processing emotional information.
   a.   left cerebral hemisphere
   b.   posterior amygdala
   c.   anterior amygdala
   d.   right cerebral hemisphere

10.15   Outward signs of others' emotional states, for example, facial expressions, are called
   a.   unconditioned responses.
   b.   nonverbal cues.
   c.   conditioned responses.
   d.   display rules.

10.16   The desire to have power, food, or sex is considered a(n)
   a.   emotion.
   b.   instinct.
   c.   motivation.
   d.   need.

10.17   Behaviors that return a person to homeostasis are likely to be repeated according to which
        of the following theories?
   a.   expectancy
   b.   drive
   c.   innate
   d.   power

10.18   Rewards individuals seek to gain are known as
  a.   expectations.
  b.   motivators.
  c.   drives.
  d.   incentives.

10.19   In the hierarchy of needs, the desire to become all that one is capable of being and to be concerned with issues that affect the well-being of others are examples of
  a.   deficiency needs.
  b.   growth needs.
  c.   self-actualization needs.
  d.   humanitarian needs.

10.20   Research indicates that _____ provides an answer as to why the short-term sexual strategies of males and females are different.
  a.   operant conditioning
  b.   evolutionary psychology
  c.   Goal-Setting Theory
  d.   Maslow's hierarchy

10.21   Frustration is most likely to lead to aggression when it is viewed as
  a.   unfair.
  b.   expected.
  c.   appropriate.
  d.   unappreciated.

10.22   Individuals who are high in achievement motivation tend to prefer
  a.   across-the-board pay systems.
  b.   cost-of-living pay systems.
  c.   merit-based pay systems.
  d   seniority pay systems.

10.23   Which theory of emotion suggests that you become happy as a result of noticing that you are smiling and laughing?
  a.   James-Lange
  b.   Cannon-Bard
  c.   Schachter-Singer
  d.   Opponent-process

10.24   Facial expression, eye contact, body movements, posture, and touching are examples of
  a.   negative emotional responses.
  b.   positive emotional responses.
  c.   nonverbal cues.
  d.   social signifiers.

10.25   The concept of _____ is defined as consisting of relatively mild feelings and moods.
  a.   contagion
  b.   emotion
  c.   affect
  d.   homeostasis

Chapter 10 - Practice Test Answer Justifications

10.1   Internal processes that activate, guide, and maintain behavior over time are called
   a.   This answer is incorrect because reinforcement can involve both internal and/or external consequences related to a behavior. Review page 370 in your textbook.
   b.   For more information, see page 370 in your textbook.
   c.   This answer is incorrect because instincts involve behaviors that are the same for all members of a particular species. Review page 370 in your textbook.
   d.   This answer is incorrect because emotions involve physiological and subjective reactions to situations. Review page 370 in your textbook.

10.2   One major problem with drive theory of motivation is that
   a.   For more information, see page 373 in your textbook.
   b.   This answer is incorrect because decreasing a drive is the assumption of drive theory, therefore not a problem. Review page 373 in your textbook.
   c.   This answer is incorrect because performing difficult behaviors is not a problem for drive theory. Review page 373 in your textbook.
   d.   This answer is incorrect because performing easy behaviors is not a problem for drive theory. Review page 373 in your textbook.

10.3   Arousal theories of motivation focus on an organism's efforts to
   a.   This answer is incorrect because maintenance of biological systems for survival is assumed under arousal theories. Review page 373 in your textbook.
   b.   This answer is incorrect because even though reaching a goal is important, such success does not address the arousal level of the organism. Review page 373 in your textbook.
   c.   For more information, see page 373 in your textbook.
   d.   This answer is incorrect because these accomplishments are not relevant to arousal theories. Review page 373 in your textbook.

10.4   One theory of motivation that involves an arrangement of needs from the most basic to the highest level is called
   a.   This answer is incorrect because configuration of needs does not specify the particular arrangement. Review page 376 in your textbook.
   b.   For more information, see page 376 in your textbook.
   c.   This answer is incorrect because Maslow's theory did not call the arrangement a needs pyramid. Review page 376 in your textbook.
   d.   This answer is incorrect because a scale does not address the arrangement of needs. Review page 376 in your textbook.

10.5   The Pima of Arizona are a good example of the role of _____ in the determination of one's weight.
   a.   This answer is incorrect because environmental factors alone are not the cause of Pima individuals being overweight. Review page 380 in your textbook.
   b.   This answer is incorrect because cognitive factors are not a primary cause of Pima individuals being overweight. Review page 380 in your textbook.
   c.   This answer is incorrect because social factors play a minor role in Pima individuals being overweight. Review page 380 in your textbook.
   d   For more information, see page 380 in your textbook.

10.6   In comparison to non-obese individuals, individuals who suffer from obesity seem to respond more strongly to
    a.   This answer is incorrect because reduced lipid levels would increase hunger in both obese and non-obese individuals. Review page 380 in your textbook.
    b.   This answer is incorrect because reduced glucose levels would increase hunger in both obese and non-obese individuals. Review page 380 in your textbook.
    c.   For more information, see page 380 in your textbook.
    d.   This answer is incorrect because internal hunger pangs are individualistic whether a person is obese or non-obese. Review page 380 in your textbook.

10.7   The desire to harm or injure someone else is called
    a.   For more information, see page 386 in your textbook.
    b.   This answer is incorrect because hurtful aggression is a behavior, not a desire. Review page 386 in your textbook.
    c.   This answer is incorrect because injurious aggression is a behavior, not a desire. Review page 386 in your textbook.
    d.   This answer is incorrect because aggression compulsion implies an abnormal behavior. Review page 386 in your textbook.

10.8   Ralph experienced _____ when he was in a hurry to get to his job interview, but found that his route was blocked by a long line of rail cars.
    a.   This answer is incorrect because conflagration is defined as an intense fire. Review page 387 in your textbook.
    b.   For more information, see page 387 in your textbook.
    c.   This answer is incorrect because aggression might have been the result of Ralph's being blocked, but not what he experienced at the time of the blockage. Review page 387 in your textbook.
    d.   This answer is incorrect because contagion involves the spreading of attributes or characteristics. Review page 387 in your textbook.

10.9   Violent outbursts in which employees attack and even kill employees colleagues is called
    a.   For more information, see page 387 in your textbook.
    b.   This answer is incorrect because workplace provocation does not characterize the resulting behavior. Review page 387 in your textbook.
    c.   This answer is incorrect because colleague violence does not give an indication where the violence occurs. Review page 387 in your textbook.
    d.   This answer is incorrect because employee violence does not encompass the entire workplace situation. Review page 387 in your textbook.

10.10   Since Lisa is always trying to succeed in the tasks she undertakes, she would be classified as high in
    a.   For more information, see page 390 in your textbook.
    b.   This answer is incorrect because such motivation involves wanting to be with people. Review page 390 in your textbook.
    c.   This answer is incorrect because such motivation would involve wanting to spread some attribute or characteristic. Review page 390 in your textbook.
    d.   This answer is incorrect because such motivation is not the name of the behavior described. Review page 390 in your textbook.

10.11 Ralph is high in _____ since he plays the piano because he likes to play the piano.
  a. This answer is incorrect because altruistic motivation would involve the desire to help someone. Review page 394 in your textbook.
  b. This answer is incorrect because extrinsic motivation would involve the desire to receive some recognition for playing the piano. Review page 394 in your textbook.
  c. This answer is incorrect because music motivation does not describe why Ralph plays the piano. Review page 394 in your textbook.
  d. For more information, see page 394 in your textbook.

10.12 Lisa truly enjoys reading. If given money for reading at a certain rate, her reading performance will likely
  a. This answer is incorrect because she would be changed from intrinsic to extrinsic motivation and her performance would be reduced. Review page 394 in your textbook.
  b. This answer is incorrect because she would be changed from intrinsic to extrinsic motivation and would read just to get the money not for the pleasure of reading. Review page 394 in your textbook.
  c. For more information, see page 394 in your textbook.
  d. This answer is incorrect because changing from intrinsic to extrinsic will probably not have an effect on what she reads. Review page 394 in your textbook.

10.13 Providing a ready excuse for potentially poor performance is called
  a. This answer is incorrect because lying does not describe the reason for providing the excuse. Review page 395 in your textbook.
  b. This answer is incorrect because deception does not describe the reason for providing the excuse. Review page 395 in your textbook.
  c. For more information, see page 395 in your textbook.
  d. This answer is incorrect because self-serving does not give any information about the reason for providing the excuse. Review page 395 in your textbook.

10.14 It appears that the _____ seems to be specialized for processing emotional information.
  a. This answer is incorrect because this hemisphere is specialized for processing non-emotional information. Review page 399 in your textbook.
  b. This answer is incorrect because the amygdala is involved in the ability to judge the intensity of others' emotions. Review page 399 in your textbook.
  c. This answer is incorrect because the amygdala is involved in the ability to judge the intensity of others' emotions. Review page 399 in your textbook.
  d. For more information, see page 399 in your textbook.

10.15 Outward signs of others' emotional states, for example, facial expressions, are called
  a. This answer is incorrect because facial expressions are not necessarily the result of any unconditioned stimulus. Review page 401 in your textbook.
  b. For more information, see page 401 in your textbook.
  c. This answer is incorrect because facial expressions are not necessarily the result of any conditioned stimulus. Review page 401 in your textbook.
  d. This answer is incorrect because display rules involve the regulation of expressions in order to communicate. Review page 401 in your textbook.

10.16 The desire to have power, food, or sex is considered a(n)
  a. This answer is incorrect because emotion is not necessarily related to desire. Review page 372 in your textbook.
  b. This answer is incorrect because an instinct specifies a particular type of behavior, not a desire. Review page 372 in your textbook.
  c. For more information, see page 372 in your textbook.
  d. This answer is incorrect because a need is something that is necessary for survival. Review page 372 in your textbook..

10.17 Behaviors that return a person to homeostasis are likely to be repeated according to which
of the following theories?

    a.   This answer is incorrect because expectancy theory does not involve homeostasis. Review page 373 in your textbook.

    b.   For more information, see page 373 in your textbook.

    c.   This answer is incorrect because innate behaviors may or may not bring an organism to homeostasis. Review page 373 in your textbook.

    d.   This answer is incorrect because power theory is not relevant to this question. Review page 373 in your textbook.

10.18 Rewards individuals seek to gain are known as

    a.   This answer is incorrect because expectations are individualized cognitive operations, which give the rewards their strength. Review page 374 in your textbook.

    b.   This answer is incorrect because motivators are those things that push an individual to respond. Review page 374 in your textbook..

    c.   This answer is incorrect because drives are those things that push an organism to respond. Review page 374 in your textbook.

    d.   For more information, see page 374 in your textbook.

10.19 In the hierarchy of needs, the desire to become all that one is capable of being and to be
concerned with issues that affect the well-being of others are examples of

    a.   This answer is incorrect because deficiency needs consist of three other lower level needs. Review page 376 in your textbook.

    b.   This answer is incorrect because growth needs consist of two other higher level needs. Review page 376 in your textbook.

    c.   For more information, see page 376 in your textbook.

    d.   This answer is incorrect because humanitarian needs are not part of Maslow's hierarchy of needs. Review page 376 in your textbook.

10.20 Research indicates that _____ provides an answer as to why the short-term sexual strategies of males
and females are different.

    a.   This answer is incorrect because operant conditioning would be related to increase or decrease of sexual strategy behavior, but not the actual strategy. Review page 383 in your textbook.

    b.   For more information, see page 383 in your textbook.

    c.   This answer is incorrect because Goal-Setting Theory would not necessarily be different for males and females. Review page 383 in your textbook.

    d.   This answer is incorrect because Maslow's hierarchy is not relevant to sexual strategies. Review page 383 in your textbook.

10.21 Frustration is most likely to lead to aggression when it is viewed as

    a.   For more information, see page 387 in your textbook.

    b.   This answer is incorrect because when frustration is expected someone can plan to respond in more appropriate ways. Review page 387 in your textbook..

    c.   This answer is incorrect because if frustration is appropriate other responses can be developed. Review page 387 in your textbook.

    d.   This answer is incorrect because unappreciated frustration is not relevant. Review page 387 in your textbook.

10.22   Individuals who are high in achievement motivation tend to prefer
  a.   This answer is incorrect because across-the-board pay systems would not recognize individual efforts. Review page 392 in your textbook.
  b.   This answer is incorrect because cost-of-living pay systems would not recognize individual efforts. Review page 392 in your textbook.
  c.   For more information, see page 392 in your textbook.
  d   This answer is incorrect because seniority pay systems would reward individuals who are not necessarily the highest producers. Review page 392 in your textbook.

10.23   Which theory of emotion suggests that you become happy as a result of noticing that you are smiling and laughing?
  a.   For more information, see page 396 in your textbook.
  b.   This answer is incorrect because the Cannon-Bard theory suggests that the laughter and the emotion of happiness would occur at the same time. Review page 396 in your textbook.
  c.   This answer is incorrect because the Schachter-Singer theory suggests that happiness is a result of arousal and social situation interpretation. Review page 396 in your textbook.
  d.   This answer is incorrect because Opponent-process theory is related to perception. Review page 396 in your textbook.

10.24   Facial expression, eye contact, body movements, posture, and touching are examples of
  a.   This answer is incorrect because such responses could be negative emotional responses or positive emotional responses. Review page 401 in your textbook.
  b.   This answer is incorrect because such responses could be positive emotional responses or negative emotional responses. Review page 401 in your textbook.
  c.   For more information, see page 401 in your textbook.
  d.   This answer is incorrect because social signifiers are not related to these responses. Review page 401 in your textbook.

10.25   The concept of _____ is defined as consisting of relatively mild feelings and moods.
  a.   This answer is incorrect because contagion involves the emotion that several individuals have from interacting with one another. Review page 403 in your textbook.
  b.   This answer is incorrect because emotion can involve both mild and more extreme feelings and moods. Review page 403 in your textbook.
  c.   For more information, see page 403 in your textbook.
  d.   This answer is incorrect because homeostasis is a physical process of balancing the systems of the body. Review page 403 in your textbook.

Chapter 10 - Practice Test Answers

Question	Answer
10.1	b
10.2	a
10.3	c
10.4	b
10.5	d
10.6	c
10.7	a
10.8	b
10.9	a
10.10	a
10.11	d
10.12	c
10.13	c
10.14	d
10.15	b
10.16	c
10.17	b
10.18	d
10.19	c
10.20	b
10.21	a
10.22	c
10.23	a
10.24	c
10.25	c

Chapter 11 - Practice Test

11.1 Spearman felt that intelligence consisted of
   a. a general ability to reason and solve problems.
   b. multiple types of intelligence.
   c. a composite of seven primary mental abilities.
   d. culturally determined skills.

11.2 In Sternberg's triarchic theory, the ability to formulate new ideas or to combine seemingly unrelated facts is referred to as
   a. componential intelligence.
   b. experiential intelligence.
   c. contextual intelligence.
   d. crystallized intelligence.

11.3 Intelligence that largely involves our inherited abilities to think and reason is called
   a. crystallized intelligence.
   b. componential intelligence.
   c. contextual intelligence.
   d. fluid intelligence.

11.4 Probably the most traditional, widely used intelligence test in recent decades has been the
   a. Stanford-Binet intelligence test.
   b. Wechsler Adult Intelligence Scale.
   c. Kaufmann Assessment Battery.
   d. Minnesota Multiphasic Measurement Scale.

11.5 Originally, IQ was derived by
   a. multiplying mental age by chronological age and dividing by 100.
   b. dividing mental age by chronological age and multiplying by 100.
   c. dividing chronological age by mental age and multiplying by 100.
   d. multiplying chronological age by mental age and dividing by 100.

11.6 Lisa was classified as _____ because she had below-average intellectual functioning combined with varying egrees of difficulty meeting the demands of everyday life.
   a. mentally challenged
   b. intellectually challenged
   c. intellectually gifted
   d. mentally retarded

11.7 You would expect practice effects to most likely to be a problem when determining
   a. split-half reliability.
   b. content validity.
   c. test-retest reliability.
   d. objectivity.

11.8 The extent to which a test measures what it actually claims to measure is the definition of
   a. reliability.
   b. validity.
   c. computability.
   d. predictability.

1.9   Recent research has found that long inspection times are closely related to _____ as measured by standard intelligence tests.
   a.   decreased intelligence
   b.   increased intelligence
   c.   decreased verbal intelligence
   d.   increased verbal intelligence

11.10   Recent research has found that the measure of _____ is negatively correlated with intelligence.
   a.   inspection time
   b.   cognitive speed
   c.   contagion time
   d.   detection time

11.11   What has happened to IQ scores worldwide during recent decades?
   a.   They have decreased significantly.
   b.   They have not changed significantly.
   c.   They have increased significantly.
   d.   They initially increased and are now decreasing significantly.

11.12   Compared with girls, boys score higher on tests of
   a.   spatial visualization.
   b.   vocabulary.
   c.   perceptual speed.
   d.   spelling.

11.13   Ralph has the ability to recognize and manage his own emotions, and is quite adept at handling interpersonal relationships. He would score high on
   a.   componential intelligence.
   b.   tacit intelligence
   c.   practical intelligence
   d.   emotional intelligence

11.14   Which one of the following resources is **not** one of the resources listed by Lubart (1994) as being part of creativity?
   a.   personality attributes
   b.   analytical style
   c.   intrinsic, task-focused motivation
   d.   supportive environment

11.15   One way to deal with anger is to laugh. It is almost impossible to be angry when you are laughing. This approach is called the
   a.   laugh-cry approach.
   b.   humorous response approach.
   c.   incompatible response approach.
   d.   emotional dissonance approach.

11.16   An individual's ability to understand complex ideas, to adapt effectively to the environment, to learn from experience, to engage in various forms of reasoning, and to overcome obstacles by careful thought is the definition of
   a.   cognition.
   b.   intelligence.
   c.   development.
   d.   personality.

11.17   According to Sternberg's triarchic theory, people who have practical sense have _____ intelligence.
a.   componential
b.   experiential
c.   contextual
d.   intuitive

11.18   One of the difficulties with the intelligence tests designed by Binet is the concentration on
a.   verbal abilities.
b.   nonverbal abilities.
c.   performance abilities.
d.   social abilities.

11.19   A multiple choice test that you take for this class is an _____ test.
a.   aptitude
b.   achievement
c.   applied
d.   acquisitions

11.20   Which one of the following is **not** one of the three crucial requirements that must be met before a test can be considered an accurate and useful test of intelligence?
a.   reliable
b.   logical
c.   standardized
d.   valid

11.21   If you develop a test to measure good study skills and when evaluated, it is determined that it actually measures good study skills, the test is said to be
a.   valid.
b.   standardized.
c.   reliable.
d.   objective.

11.22   The correlation between two identical twins raised together is almost
a.   -.30.
b.   +.30.
c.   -.90.
d.   +.90.

11.23   Compared with girls, boys score higher on tests of
a.   reading.
b.   spelling.
c.   mental rotation.
d.   writing.

11.24   The type of intelligence that is concerned with the ability to recognize and manage emotions, restrain impulses, and handle interpersonal relationships effectively is called
a.   impulsive intelligence.
b.   interpersonal intelligence.
c.   emotional intelligence.
d.   cognitive intelligence.

11.25 The ability to create work that is novel and appropriate is called _____.
    a. creativity
    b. productivity
    c. originality
    d. novelty

Chapter 11- Practice Test Answer Justifications

11.1   Spearman felt that intelligence consisted of
    a.   For more information, see page 414 in your textbook.
    b.   This answer is incorrect because this was the position adopted by Thurstone. Review page 414 in your textbook.
    c.   This answer is incorrect because this approach involves factor analysis that leads to more than one specific factor. Review page 414 in your textbook.
    d.   This answer is incorrect because this definition is the basis for types of tests, not Spearman's definition of intelligence. Review page 414 in your textbook.

11.2   In Sternberg's triarchic theory, the ability to formulate new ideas or to combine seemingly unrelated facts is referred to as
    a.   This answer is incorrect because this type of intelligence involves the ability to think critically and analytically. Review page 415 in your textbook.
    b.   For more information, see page 415 in your textbook.
    c.   This answer is incorrect because this type of intelligence involves the ability to solve the problems of everyday life. Review page 415 in your textbook.
    d.   This answer is incorrect because this is a type of intelligence derived from factor analysis. Review page 415 in your textbook.

11.3   Intelligence that is largely involves our inherited abilities to think and reason is called
    a.   This answer is incorrect because this type of intelligence involves accumulated knowledge acquired from experience. Review page 416 in your textbook.
    b.   This answer is incorrect because this intelligence involves the ability to think critically and analytically. Review page 416 in your textbook.
    c.   This answer is incorrect because this intelligence involves the practical solution of problems. Review page 416 in your textbook.
    d.   For more information, see page 416 in your textbook.

11.4   Probably the most traditional, widely used intelligence test for children in recent decades has been the
    a.   For more information, see page 416 in your textbook.
    b.   This answer is incorrect because this scale measures adult intelligence. Review page 416 in your textbook.
    c.   This answer is incorrect because this test battery is relatively new and is not traditional. Review page 416 in your textbook.
    d.   This answer is incorrect because this scale measures personality. Review page 416 in your textbook.

11.5   Originally, IQ was derived by
    a.   This answer is incorrect because this formula would not result in a traditional IQ score. Review page 417 in your textbook.
    b.   For more information, see page 417 in your textbook.
    c.   This answer is incorrect because this formula would not result in a traditional IQ score. Review page 417 in your textbook.
    d.   This answer is incorrect because this formula would not result in a traditional IQ score. Review page 417 in your textbook.

11.6   Lisa was classified as _____ because she had below-average intellectual functioning combined with varying degrees of difficulty meeting the demands of everyday life.
a.   This answer is incorrect because this is not a descriptive category. Review page 419 in your textbook.
b.   This answer is incorrect because this is not a descriptive category. Review page 419 in your textbook.
c.   This answer is incorrect because her performance indicated below-average intelligence. Review page 419 in your textbook.
d.   For more information, see page 419 in your textbook.

11.7   You would expect practice effects to most likely to be a problem when determining
a.   This answer is incorrect because such a determination could be made at one time. Review page 423 in your textbook.
b.   This answer is incorrect because such a determination could be made at one time. Review page 423 in your textbook.
c.   For more information, see page 423 in your textbook.
d.   This answer is incorrect because this test characteristic is not dependent upon time. Review page 423 in your textbook.

11.8   The extent to which a test measures what it actually claims to measure is the definition of
a.   This answer is incorrect because reliability involves consistency of scores over time. Review page 423 in your textbook.
b.   For more information, see page 423 in your textbook.
c.   This answer is incorrect because computability does not involve measurement accuracy. Review page 423 in your textbook.
d.   This answer is incorrect because predictability involves the future not just measurement accuracy. Review page 423 in your textbook.

11.9   Recent research has found that long inspection times are closely related to _____ as measured by standard intelligence tests.
a.   For more information, see page 425 in your textbook.
b.   This answer is incorrect because there is a negative relationship between inspection time and intelligence. Review page 425 in your textbook.
c.   This answer is incorrect because the relationship between inspection time and verbal intelligence has not been established. Review page 425 in your textbook.
d.   This answer is incorrect because the relationship between inspection time and verbal intelligence has not been established. Review page 425 in your textbook.

11.10   Recent research has found that the measure of _____ is negatively correlated with intelligence.
a.   For more information, see page 425 in your textbook.
b.   This answer is incorrect because cognitive speed has not been directly measured. Review page 425 in your textbook.
c.   This answer is incorrect because contagion involves spreading of attributes, not intelligence. Review page 425 in your textbook.
d.   This answer is incorrect because detection time involves the speed to detect a stimulus, not process information. Review page 425 in your textbook.

11.11   What has happened to IQ scores worldwide during recent decades?
a.   This answer is incorrect because IQ scores have increased about 3 points per decade. Review page 431 in your textbook.
b.   This answer is incorrect because IQ scores have increased about 3 points per decade. Review page 431 in your textbook.
c.   For more information, see page 431 in your textbook.
d.   This answer is incorrect because IQ scores have increased about 3 points per decade. Review page 431 in your textbook.

11.12   Compared with girls, boys score higher on tests of
    a.   For more information, see page 437 in your textbook.
    b.   This answer is incorrect because girls tend to score higher on this characteristic. Review page 437 in your textbook.
    c.   This answer is incorrect because there are essentially no differences in this characteristic. Review page 437 in your textbook.
    d.   This answer is incorrect because spelling is related to vocabulary, on which girls score higher. Review page 437 in your textbook.

11.13   Ralph has the ability to recognize and manage his own emotions, and is quite adept at handling interpersonal relationships. He would score high on
    a.   This answer is incorrect because this type of intelligence does not include the behaviors listed. Review page 439 in your textbook.
    b.   This answer is incorrect because this type of intelligence does not include the behaviors listed. Review page 439 in your textbook.
    c.   This answer is incorrect because this type of intelligence does not include the behaviors listed. Review page 439 in your textbook.
    d.   For more information, see page 439 in your textbook.

11.14   Which one of the following resources is **not** one of the resources listed by Lubart (1994) as being part of creativity?
    a.   This answer is incorrect because this resource is one of those listed. Review page 444 in your textbook.
    b.   For more information, see page 444 in your textbook.
    c.   This answer is incorrect because this resource is one of those listed. Review page 444 in your textbook.
    d.   This answer is incorrect because this resource is one of those listed. Review page 444 in your textbook.

11.15   One way to deal with anger is to laugh. It is almost impossible to be angry when you are laughing. This approach is called the
    a.   This answer is incorrect because this is not the name of the approach being illustrated. Review page 445 in your textbook.
    b.   This answer is incorrect because this is not the name of the approach being illustrated. Review page 445 in your textbook.
    c.   For more information, see page 445 in your textbook.
    d.   This answer is incorrect because this is not the name of the approach being illustrated. Review page 445 in your textbook.

11.16   An individual's ability to understand complex ideas, to adapt effectively to the environment, to learn from experience, to engage in various forms of reasoning, and to overcome obstacles by careful thought is the definition of
    a.   This answer is incorrect because cognition is defined in a much more limited way. Review page 413 in your textbook.
    b.   For more information, see page 413 in your textbook.
    c.   This answer is incorrect because development includes physical, social, emotional, moral, etc. development, which are not mentioned. Review page 413 in your textbook.
    d.   This answer is incorrect because personality involves consistency of behavior and is more limited in definition. Review page 413 in your textbook.

11.17 According to Sternberg's triarchic theory, people who have practical sense have _____ intelligence.
  a. This answer is incorrect because componential intelligence involves the ability to think critically. Review page 415 in your textbook.
  b. This answer is incorrect because experiential intelligence involves the ability to generate new ideas. Review page 415 in your textbook.
  c. For more information, see page 415 in your textbook.
  d. This answer is incorrect because intuitive intelligence is not a part of Sternberg's theory. Review page 415 in your textbook.

11.18 One of the difficulties with the intelligence tests designed by Binet is the concentration on
  a. For more information, see page 417 in your textbook.
  b. This answer is incorrect because nonverbal abilities were not emphasized. Review page 417 in your textbook.
  c. This answer is incorrect because performance abilities were not emphasized. Review page 417 in your textbook.
  d. This answer is incorrect because social abilities were not included. Review page 417 in your textbook.

11.19 A multiple choice test that you take for this class is an _____ test.
  a. This answer is incorrect because an aptitude test predicts future behavior. Review page 419 in your textbook.
  b. For more information, see page 419 in your textbook.
  c. This answer is incorrect because these questions are not applied or practical type of questions. Review page 419 in your textbook.
  d. This answer is incorrect because acquisitions is not a type of test. Review page 419 in your textbook.

11.20 Which one of the following is **not** one of the three crucial requirements that must be met before a test can be considered an accurate and useful test of intelligence?
  a. This answer is incorrect because reliable or reliability is a requirement. Review page 422 in your textbook.
  b. For more information, see page 422 in your textbook.
  c. This answer is incorrect because standard or standardization is a requirement. Review page 422 in your textbook.
  d. This answer is incorrect because valid or validity is a requirement. Review page 422 in your textbook.

11.21 If you develop a test to measure good study skills and when evaluated, it is determined that it actually measures good study skills, the test is said to be
  a. For more information, see page 423 in your textbook.
  b. This answer is incorrect because standardized means to give the test in a particular way or norm it on representative individuals. Review page 423 in your textbook.
  c. This answer is incorrect because to be reliable, the test must consistently. Review page 423 in your textbook.
  d. This answer is incorrect because if the test yields the same scores for individuals responding in the same way, the test is objective. Review page 423 in your textbook.

11.22 The correlation between the intelligence of two identical twins raised together is almost
  a. This answer is incorrect because -.30 is a weak, negative relationship, which does not reflect reality. Review page 428 in your textbook.
  b. This answer is incorrect because +.30 is a weak, positive relationship, which does not reflect reality. Review page 428 in your textbook.
  c. This answer is incorrect because -.90 indicates a strong, negative relationship, which does not reflect reality. Review page 428 in your textbook.
  d. For more information, see page 428 in your textbook.

11.23 Compared with girls, boys score higher on tests of
   a. This answer is incorrect because there is a slight difference favoring girls in reading, reflecting their overall higher verbal abilities. Review page 437 in your textbook.
   b. This answer is incorrect because girls tend to score higher on spelling, which indicates their overall higher verbal abilities. Review page 437 in your textbook.
   c. For more information, see page 437 in your textbook.
   d. This answer is incorrect because girls tend to score higher in writing, indicating their overall higher verbal abilities. Review page 437 in your textbook.

11.24 The type of intelligence that is concerned with the ability to recognize and manage emotions, restrain impulses, and handle interpersonal relationships effectively is called
   a. This answer is incorrect because impulsive intelligence does not exist. Review page 440 in your textbook.
   b. This answer is incorrect because interpersonal intelligence does not exist. Review page 440 in your textbook.
   c. For more information, see page 440 in your textbook.
   d. This answer is incorrect because cognitive intelligence is not directly related to interpersonal relationships. Review page 440 in your textbook.

11.25 The ability to create work that is novel and appropriate is called _____.
   a. For more information, see page 442 in your textbook.
   b. This answer is incorrect because productivity is not necessarily related to novel work. Review page 442 in your textbook.
   c. This answer is incorrect because originality is not necessarily related to appropriate work. Review page 442 in your textbook.
   d. This answer is incorrect because novelty is not necessarily related to appropriate work. Review page 442 in your textbook.

104

Chapter 11 - Practice Test Answers

Question	Answer
11.1	a
11.2	b
11.3	d
11.4	a
11.5	b
11.6	d
11.7	c
11.8	b
11.9	a
11.10	a
11.11	c
11.12	a
11.13	d
11.14	b
11.15	c
11.16	b
11.17	c
11.18	a
11.19	b
11.20	b
11.21	a
11.22	d
11.23	c
11.24	c
11.25	a

Chapter 12 - Practice Test

12.1   The definition of the term personality includes
    a.   idiosyncratic characteristics that change over time.
    b.   features for which no measurement devices exist.
    c.   unique and relatively stable features.
    d.   inconsistent features that change with environmental pressures.

12.2   The _____ is made up of the thoughts, desires, and impulses of which we are largely unaware.
    a.   conscious
    b.   subconscious
    c.   preconscious
    d.   unconscious

12.3   The part of the personality that takes into account external reality in the expression of instinctual urges is the
    a.   ego.
    b.   superego.
    c.   id.
    d.   libido.

12.4   The defense mechanism of sublimation involves
    a.   putting your own feelings onto someone else.
    b.   finding a socially acceptable outlet for your feelings.
    c.   thinking of a logical, rational excuse for doing what you want.
    d.   adopting behaviors that are the opposite of your true feelings.

12.5   According to Freud, too little or too much gratification during the psychosexual stages of development can result in psychic energy being left behind in one of the stages. This process is referred to as
    a.   repression.
    b.   fixation.
    c.   ego transference.
    d.   id transference.

12.6   According to Jung, the inherited manifestations of the collective unconscious that shape our perceptions of the external world are
    a.   archetypes.
    b.   secondary traits.
    c.   central traits.
    d.   cardinal traits.

12.7   One of the factors Alfred Adler believed to be important in shaping personality is
    a.   difficulty with toilet training.
    b.   birth order within a family.
    c.   unconditional positive regard.
    d.   the collective unconscious.

12.8   One of the major characteristics of humanistic psychology is each individual's motivation to
    a.   defend against unconscious anxiety.
    b.   achieve personal growth.
    c.   overcome inferiority and achieve superiority.
    d.   secure reinforcement and avoid punishment.

12.9   Rogers suggested that healthy development can occur if an individual develops in an atmosphere
consisting of
    a.   unconditional negative regard.
    b.   conditional negative regard.
    c.   conditional positive regard.
    d.   unconditional positive regard.

12.10   In Maslow's theory of personality, a peak experience generally includes feelings of
    a.   power, wonder, and unity with the universe.
    b.   anxiety as id impulses threaten to break free.
    c.   separation between the aspects of personality.
    d.   power and control over other people.

12.11   Lisa learned to read because her mother wanted her to read. Later in life, Lisa reads for her own pleasure.
According to Allport, this situation illustrates
    a.   functional autonomy.
    b.   positive regard.
    c.   self-actualization.
    d.   agreeableness.

12.12   An individual who is high on the "big five" trait of _____, but low on neuroticism would probably make a
good leader.
    a.   conscientiousness
    b.   extraversion
    c.   emotional stability.
    d.   openness to experience

12.13   The belief in one's ability to perform a task successfully is called:
    a.   self-concept.
    b.   self-actualization.
    c.   self-efficacy.
    d.   self-esteem.

12.14   A test with clinical scales that include hypochondriasis, paranoia, hypomania, and
psychasthenia is the
    a.   Rorschach Ink Blot Test.
    b.   16 Personality Factor Questionnaire (16PF).
    c.   California Personality Inventory (CPI).
    d.   Minnesota Multiphasic Personality Inventory (MMPI-2).

12.15   Someone who is high in sensation seeking is probably someone whose nervous system
    a.   was exposed to dangerous drugs before birth.
    b.   is particularly unable to deal well with stress.
    c.   operates best at a high level of arousal.
    d.   is no different from anyone else's nervous system.

12.16   According to Freud, the bulk of the mind resided in the
        a.   preconscious.
        b.   unconscious.
        c.   conscious.
        d.   superego.

12.17   According to Freud, the part of our mind that includes various bodily needs, sexual desires,
        and aggressive impulses is the
        a.   ego.
        b.   id.
        c.   superego.
        d.   conscience.

12.18   According to Freud, which of the following represents our internalization of our parents'
        moral teachings and norms of society?
        a.   superego
        b.   id
        c.   ego
        d.   morality principle

12.19   Psychosexual stages are structured by the fact that, as we grow, different parts of the body
        serve as the focus of the id's constant quest for
        a.   pleasure.
        b.   self-actualization.
        c.   anxiety.
        d.   attachment.

12.20   According to Jung, the store of ideas that we inherit from our ancestors that is a part of our
        biological heritage is the
        a.   personal unconscious.
        b.   Oedipal crisis.
        c.   collective unconscious.
        d.   psychic memory.

12.21   According to Alfred Adler, the major force that drives a person's personality is
        a.   inferiority.
        b.   pleasure.
        c.   sex.
        d.   aggression.

12.22   A form of therapy developed by Carl Rogers is
        a.   psychoanalysis.
        b.   systematic desensitization.
        c.   rational-emotive therapy.
        d.   client-centered therapy.

12.23   Which of the following is not one of the five key dimensions of personality identified by
        recent research?
        a.   extraversion
        b.   agreeableness
        c.   intelligence
        d.   conscientiousness

12.24   In Bandura's theory, our perceived ability to carry out a desired action is called
      a.   self-reinforcement.
      b.   self-efficacy.
      c.   self-regulation.
      d.   self-esteem.

12.25   Which of the following theories is based on widely-accepted principles for which there is an impressive amount of empirical evidence?
      a.   humanistic
      b.   psychoanalytic
      c.   learning
      d.   neo-Freudian

Chapter 12 - Practice Test Answer Justifications

12.1 The definition of the term personality includes
   a. This answer is incorrect because personality emphasizes consistency. Review page 450 in your textbook.
   b. This answer is incorrect because personality measures do exist. Review page 450 in your textbook.
   c. For more information, see page 450 in your textbook.
   d. This answer is incorrect because personality emphasizes consistency. Review page 450 in your textbook.

12.2 The _____ is made up of the thoughts, desires, and impulses of which we are largely unaware.
   a. This answer is incorrect because the conscious includes our current thoughts. Review page 453 in your textbook.
   b. This answer is incorrect because the subconscious was not a part of Freud's arrangement. Review page 453 in your textbook.
   c. This answer is incorrect because the preconscious includes those thoughts that can be readily brought to consciousness. Review page 453 in your textbook.
   d. For more information, see page 453 in your textbook.

12.3 The part of the personality that takes into account external reality in the expression of instinctual urges is the
   a. For more information, see page 455 in your textbook.
   b. This answer is incorrect because the superego represents morality. Review page 455 in your textbook.
   c. This answer is incorrect because the id represents primitive, innate urges. Review page 455 in your textbook.
   d. This answer is incorrect because the libido represents instinctual life force. Review page 455 in your textbook.

12.4 The defense mechanism of sublimation involves
   a. This answer is incorrect because the defense mechanism of projection is being described. Review page 456 in your textbook.
   b. For more information, see page 456 in your textbook.
   c. This answer is incorrect because the defense mechanism of rationalism is being described. Review page 456 in your textbook.
   d. This answer is incorrect because the defense mechanism of displacement is being described. Review page 456 in your textbook.

12.5 According to Freud, too little or too much gratification during the psychosexual stages of development can result in psychic energy being left behind in one of the stages. This process is referred to as
   a. This answer is incorrect because repression involves exhibiting behaviors from a previous developmental stage. Review page 457 in your textbook.
   b. For more information, see page 457 in your textbook.
   c. This answer is incorrect because ego transference is involved in psychotherapy. Review page 457 in your textbook.
   d. This answer is incorrect because id transference is involved in psychotherapy. Review page 457 in your textbook

12.6   According to Jung, the inherited manifestations of the collective unconscious that shape our perceptions of the external world are
    a.   For more information, see page 462 in your textbook.
    b.   This answer is incorrect because such traits are part of trait theory, not the unconscious. Review page 462 in your textbook.
    c.   This answer is incorrect because such traits are part of trait theory, not the unconscious. Review page 462 in your textbook.
    d.   This answer is incorrect because such traits are part of trait theory, not the unconscious. Review page 462 in your textbook.

12.7   One of the factors Alfred Adler believed to be important in shaping personality is
    a.   This answer is incorrect because toilet training was a part of Freudian theory. Review page 463 in your textbook.
    b.   For more information, see page 463 in your textbook.
    c.   This answer is incorrect because positive regard was a part of Rogers' theory. Review page 463 in your textbook.
    d.   This answer is incorrect because collective unconscious was a part of Jung's theory. Review page 463 in your textbook.

12.8   One of the major characteristics of humanistic psychology is each individual's motivation to
    a.   This answer is incorrect because unconscious anxiety is a part of Freudian theory. Review page 464 in your textbook.
    b.   For more information, see page 464 in your textbook.
    c.   This answer is incorrect because these activities are part of Adler's theory. Review page 464 in your textbook.
    d.   This answer is incorrect because these activities are part of behavioristic theory. Review page 464 in your textbook.

12.9   Rogers suggested that healthy development can occur if an individual develops in an atmosphere consisting of
    a.   This answer is incorrect because this atmosphere would not accept any individual. Review page 465 in your textbook.
    b.   This answer is incorrect because this atmosphere would emphasize not accepting an individual only when that person did behave in usually acceptable ways. Review page 465 in your textbook.
    c.   This answer is incorrect because this atmosphere would emphasize accepting an individual only when that person did behave in an certain acceptable way. Review page 465 in your textbook.
    d.   For more information, see page 465 in your textbook.

12.10   In Maslow's theory of personality, a peak experience generally includes feelings of
    a.   For more information, see page 465 in your textbook.
    b.   This answer is incorrect because the id is not a part of Maslow's theory. Review page 465 in your textbook.
    c.   This answer is incorrect because Maslow's theory emphasizes unity of personality. Review page 465 in your textbook.
    d.   This answer is incorrect because Maslow's theory would not emphasize power over other people. Review page 465 in your textbook.

12.11   Lisa learned to read because her mother wanted her to read. Later in life, Lisa reads for her own pleasure. According to Allport, this situation illustrates
a.   For more information, see page 469 in your textbook.
b.   This answer is incorrect because positive regard is not part of Allport's theory. Review page 469 in your textbook.
c.   This answer is incorrect because self-actualization is part of Rogers' and of Maslow's theory. Review page 469 in your textbook.
d.   This answer is incorrect because agreeableness is part of the "Bog five" personality theory. Review page 469 in your textbook.

12.12   An individual who is high on the "big five" trait of _____, but low on neuroticism would probably make a good leader.
a.   This answer is incorrect because conscientiousness is not necessarily involved in leadership. Review page 471 in your textbook.
b.   For more information, see page 471 in your textbook.
c.   This answer is incorrect because the degree of emotional stability is not a predictor of leadership ability. Review page 471 in your textbook.
d.   This answer is incorrect because this characteristic is not associated with leadership. Review page 471 in your textbook.

12.13   The belief in one's ability to perform a task successfully is called
a.   This answer is incorrect because self-concept is not necessarily related to performance of a specific task. Review page 473 in your textbook.
b.   This answer is incorrect because self-actualization is not related to performance of a specific task. Review page 473 in your textbook.
c.   For more information, see page 473 in your textbook.
d.   This answer is incorrect because self-esteem is not necessarily related to performance of a specific task. Review page 473 in your textbook.

12.14   A test with clinical scales that include hypochondriasis, paranoia, hypomania, and psychasthenia is the
a.   This answer is incorrect because this test gives a global score, and does not have specific clinical scales. Review page 477 in your textbook.
b.   This answer is incorrect because this questionnaire does not yield scores on clinical scales. Review page 477 in your textbook.
c.   This answer is incorrect because this inventory does not yield scores on clinical scales. Review page 477 in your textbook.
d.   For more information, see page 477 in your textbook.

12.15   Someone who is high in sensation seeking is probably someone whose nervous system
a.   This answer is incorrect because such a condition would not necessarily influence the occurrence of sensation seeking. Review page 481 in your textbook.
b.   This answer is incorrect because a sensation seeker would have to deal with high levels of stress . Review page 481 in your textbook.
c.   For more information, see page 481 in your textbook.
d.   This answer is incorrect because the nervous system of sensation seekers have higher activity levels in the catecholamine system. Review page 481 in your textbook.

12.16 According to Freud, the bulk of the mind resided in the
   a. This answer is incorrect because the preconscious is relatively small and holds only those things readily needed. Review page 453 in your textbook.
   b. For more information, see page 453 in your textbook.
   c. This answer is incorrect because the conscious contains only those things that we are aware of at any one point in time. Review page 453 in your textbook.
   d. This answer is incorrect because the superego is essentially our conscience, which is a part of our mind. Review page 453 in your textbook.

12.17 According to Freud, the part of our mind that includes various bodily needs, sexual desires, and aggressive impulses is the
   a. This answer is incorrect because the ego mediates these activities through contact with the real world. Review page 455 in your textbook..
   b. For more information, see page 455 in your textbook.
   c. This answer is incorrect because the superego is our conscience and mediates these activities through morals and ethics. Review page 455 in your textbook.
   d. This answer is incorrect because our conscience is our superego, which mediates these activities. Review page 455 in your textbook.

12.18 According to Freud, which of the following represents our internalization of our parents' moral teachings and norms of society?
   a. For more information, see page 455 in your textbook.
   b. This answer is incorrect because the id represents impulses and innate drives. Review page 455 in your textbook.
   c. This answer is incorrect because the ego represents reality. Review page 455 in your textbook.
   d. This answer is incorrect because the morality principle is the guiding light under which the superego operatives. Review page 455 in your textbook.

12.19 Psychosexual stages are structured by the fact that, as we grow, different parts of the body serve as the focus of the id's constant quest for
   a. For more information, see page 457 in your textbook.
   b. This answer is incorrect because self-actualization is a higher level need in Maslow's theory. Review page 457 in your textbook.
   c. This answer is incorrect because anxiety is something we try to avoid. Review page 457 in your textbook.
   d. This answer is incorrect because attachment is too general a term to be related to the id's operations. Review page 457 in your textbook.

12.20 According to Jung, the store of ideas that we inherit from our ancestors that is a part of our biological heritage is the
   a. This answer is incorrect because the personal unconscious is what we develop. Review page 462 in your textbook.
   b. This answer is incorrect because the Oedipal crisis is a developmental crisis for an individual. Review page 462 in your textbook.
   c. For more information, see page 462 in your textbook.
   d. This answer is incorrect because psychic memory is not related to our biological heritage. Review page 462 in your textbook.

12.21 According to Alfred Adler, the major force that drives a person's personality is
   a. For more information, see page 463 in your textbook.
   b. This answer is incorrect because pleasure was a lessor driving force. Review page 463 in your textbook.
   c. This answer is incorrect because sex was a lesser driving force. Review page 463 in your textbook.
   d. This answer is incorrect because aggression was a lessor driving force. Review page 463 in your textbook.

12.22 A form of therapy developed by Carl Rogers is
   a. This answer is incorrect because psychoanalysis was developed by Freud. Review page 465 in your textbook.
   b. This answer is incorrect because systematic desensitization is related to classical conditioning. Review page 465 in your textbook.
   c. This answer is incorrect because rational-emotive therapy was developed by Ellis. Review page 465 in your textbook.
   d. For more information, see page 465 in your textbook.

12.23 Which of the following is **not** one of the five key dimensions of personality identified by recent research?
   a. This answer is incorrect because extraversion is one of the dimensions. Review page 470 in your textbook.
   b. This answer is incorrect because agreeablenessis one of the dimensions. Review page 470 in your textbook.
   c. For more information, see page 470 in your textbook.
   d. This answer is incorrect because conscientiousness is one of the dimensions. Review page 470 in your textbook.

12.24 In Bandura's theory, our perceived ability to carry out a desired action is called
   a. This answer is incorrect because self-reinforcement involves doing something to ourselves to increase a response. Review page 489 in your textbook.
   b. For more information, see page 489 in your textbook.
   c. This answer is incorrect because self-regulation does not involve perceived ability. Review page 489 in your textbook.
   d. This answer is incorrect because self-esteem involves how we feel about ourselves, not whether we can or cannot complete a task. Review page 489 in your textbook.

12.25 Which of the following theories is based on widely-accepted principles for which there is an impressive amount of empirical evidence?
   a. This answer is incorrect because humanistic theories are very limited in terms of the data available to support their principles, many of which are not accepted at all. Review page 475 in your textbook.
   b. This answer is incorrect because psychoanalytic theories have a paucity of data to support the principles, many of which are not accepted. Review page 475 in your textbook.
   c. For more information, see page 475 in your textbook.
   d. This answer is incorrect because neo-Freudian theories are lacking supporting data and no well-established principles. Review page 475 in your textbook.

Chapter 12 - Practice Test Answers

Question	Answer
12.1	c
12.2	d
12.3	a
12.4	b
12.5	b
12.6	a
12.7	b
12.8	b
12.9	d
12.10	a
12.11	a
12.12	b
12.13	c
12.14	d
12.15	c
12.16	b
12.17	b
12.18	a
12.19	a
12.20	c
12.21	a
12.22	d
12.23	c
12.24	b
12.25	c

Chapter 13 - Practice Test

13.1   Health psychology is the subfield of psychology that focuses on
    a.   the application of psychological variables to issues of health.
    b.   the appropriate psychological training for medical doctors.
    c.   understanding unconscious motivations that make people ill.
    d.   developing better organizational structures for hospitals.

13.2   During the resistance stage of the general adaptation syndrome, people will exhibit _____ than in the alarm stage.
    a.   more moderate, sustained levels of arousal
    b.   lower levels of arousal
    c.   higher levels of arousal
    d.   rapidly fluctuating levels of arousal

13.3   Recent evidence suggests that _____ are an important cause of stress because their low intensity occurs at a much higher frequency.
    a.   acute stressors
    b.   short duration stressors
    c.   hassles
    d.   long duration stressors

13.4   Being asked to do too many things in a short period of time is called work
    a.   conflict.
    b.   overload.
    c.   underload.
    d.   incompatibility.

13.5   Research indicates that a stress may be increased by
    a.   an enhanced affective strategy.
    b.   a social contagion situation.
    c.   a poor person-environment fit.
    d.   an elaborative cognitive mechanism.

13.6   An optimistic attitude can help reduce our experience of stress, probably because optimism leads to
    a.   engaging in behaviors that will improve the situation.
    b.   acceptance of the situation staying the way it is.
    c.   an increased level of nervous system reactance.
    d.   an ability to avoid thinking too much about the stressor.

13.7   According to the health belief model, our willingness to seek medical help depends on the
    a.   amount of role conflict in our lives.
    b.   extent to which we perceive a threat to our health.
    c.   stage of the general adaptation syndrome.
    d.   level of education earned.

13.8   Which of the following is least likely to be communicated between a doctor and a patient?
    a.   telling the patient how to take a prescription medicine
    b.   telling the patient the purpose of a specific test being given
    c.   explaining how the illness will be treated
    d.   asking the patient what he knows about the illness

13.9   According to _____, long-term weight loss maintenance is dependent upon whether there is the perception of autonomous control or external control of the motivation to lose weight.
a. self-control theory
b. self-concept theory
c. self-determination theory
d. self-actualization theory

13.10   In the Type A behavior pattern, there is a positive correlation between risk for heart risk and
a. emotional variability.
b. affective threshold.
c. physical activity.
d. cynical hostility.

13.11   One model that has been found useful for developing intervention strategies for groups of individuals thought to be at risk for HIV is
a. the intervention-behavioral-modeling (IBM) model.
b. the information-motivation-behavioral skills (IMB) model.
d. the knowledge-activity (KA) model.
d. the knowledge-practice-activity (KPA) model.

13.12   The most important factor contributing to longevity and good health seems to be
a. lack of alcohol consumption.
b. regular exercise.
c. high protein diets.
d. relatively high caloric intake.

13.13   Which of the following is **not** listed as a factor that might contribute to an extended life span?
a. regular exercise
b. continued activity in later life
c. early retirement
d. balanced, low-fat, low-calorie diet

13.14   Prevention strategies that are designed to increase early detection are called
a. preliminary.
b. tertiary.
c. primary.
d. secondary.

13.15   If an individual replaces negative appraisals of stressors with positive appraisals, that individual has engaged in
a. cognitive framing.
b. cognitive enhancement.
c. cognitive restructuring.
d. cognitive confinement.

13.16   The _____ of an individual involves the overall pattern of decisions and behaviors that determine health and quality of life.
a. lifestyle
b. cognitive structure
c. genetic makeup
d. experience

13.17   As a result of continued stress, you seem to catch every flu bug that comes around. Which
        stage of the general adaptation syndrome are you most likely to be experiencing?
        a. weakness
        b. alarm
        c. resistance
        d. exhaustion

13.18   Individuals who remain healthy even after prolonged exposure to high levels of stress are called
        a. hardy.
        b. resilient.
        c. adaptors.
        d. innovators.

13.19   Annoying minor events of everyday life that cumulatively can affect psychological well-being are called
        a. annoyances.
        b. hassles.
        c. stressors.
        d. repeats.

13.20   People who have general expectancies for poor outcomes in challenging situations are
        said to be
        a. unrealistic.
        b. delusional
        c. pessimists.
        d. exhausted.

13.21   A coping strategy that involves a set of specific steps for identifying the stressor, choosing
        a method of stress reduction, implementing the method and evaluating its success is
        a(n) _____ strategy.
        a. external
        b. internal
        c. defense-oriented
        d. problem-focused

13.22   Lifestyle features that affect our chances of becoming ill are termed _____ factors.
        a. risk
        b. carcinogen
        c. punishment
        d. individual

13.23   Which of the following is not likely to influence your decision to smoke?
        a. biological factors
        b. racial factors
        c. psychological factors
        d. cognitive factors

13.24   The _____ personality type is characterized by a general tendency to cope with stress by keeping
        negative emotions to him or her self.
        a. Type A
        b. Type D
        c. Type B
        d. Type E

13.25 Prevention strategies that are designed to increase early detection are called
   a. preliminary.
   b. tertiary.
   c. primary.
   d. secondary.

Chapter 13 - Practice Test Answer Justifications

13.1   Health psychology is the subfield of psychology that focuses on
    a.   For more information, see page 490 in your textbook.
    b.   This answer is incorrect because medical training is not a part of psychology. Review page 490 in your textbook.
    c.   This answer is incorrect because understanding unconscious motivations would be related to psychotherapy, not the general field of psychology. Review page 490 in your textbook.
    d.   This answer is incorrect because organizational structures would be related to industrial/organizational psychology, not the general field of psychology. Review page 490 in your textbook.

13.2   During the resistance stage of the general adaptation syndrome, people will exhibit _____ than in the alarm stage.
    a.   This answer is incorrect because the level of arousal is lower. Review page 495 in your textbook.
    b.   For more information, see page 495 in your textbook.
    c.   This answer is incorrect because the level of arousal is lower. Review page 495 in your textbook.
    d.   This answer is incorrect because the level of arousal is lower. Review page 495 in your textbook.

13.3   Recent evidence suggests that _____ are an important cause of stress because their low intensity occurs at a much higher frequency.
    a.   This answer is incorrect because these stressors occur with high intensity. Review page 498 in your textbook.
    b.   This answer is incorrect because these stressors may be high or low intensity stressors, but they occur for a short time. Review page 498 in your textbook.
    c.   For more information, see page 498 in your textbook.
    d.   This answer is incorrect because these stressors occur with low frequency. Review page 498 in your textbook.

13.4   Being asked to do too many things in a short period of time is called work
    a.   This answer is incorrect because conflict would probably involve other individuals. Review page 499 in your textbook.
    b.   For more information, see page 499 in your textbook.
    c.   This answer is incorrect because too much work would be an overload. Review page 499 in your textbook.
    d.   This answer is incorrect because incompatibility may not involve time. Review page 499 in your textbook.

13.5   Research indicates that a stress may be increased by
    a.   This answer is incorrect because such a strategy may be effective in one stressful situation, but not in others. Review page 500 in your textbook.
    b.   This answer is incorrect because such a situation would not necessarily be related to stress and may actually lead to a decrease in stress. Review page 500 in your textbook.
    c.   For more information, see page 500 in your textbook.
    d.   This answer is incorrect because such a mechanism would be effective in remembering material, but not dealing with stress. Review page 500 in your textbook.

13.6   An optimistic attitude can help reduce our experience of stress, probably because optimism leads to
    a.   For more information, see page 502 in your textbook.
    b.   This answer is incorrect because optimists engage in problem-focused coping. Review page 502 in your textbook.
    c.   This answer is incorrect because the nervous system would not be affected by being an optimist, but the immune system would be affected. Review page 502 in your textbook.
    d.   This answer is incorrect because optimists engage in problem-focused coping and would think about the stressor. Review page 502 in your textbook.

13.7 According to the health belief model, our willingness to seek medical help depends on the
 a. This answer is incorrect because role conflict is not a part of this model. Review page 504 in your textbook.
 b. For more information, see page 504 in your textbook.
 c. This answer is incorrect because the GAS stage is not relevant to this model. Review page 504 in your textbook.
 d. This answer is incorrect because the level of education is definitely not related to this model. Review page 504 in your textbook.

13.8 Which of the following is least likely to be communicated between a physician and a patient?
 a. This answer is incorrect because medicine is a part of the medication and therapy. Review page 505 in your textbook.
 b. This answer is incorrect because a specific test is part of the medication and therapy. Review page 505 in your textbook.
 c. This answer is incorrect because the treatment regime is part of medication and therapy. Review page 505 in your textbook.
 d. For more information, see page 505 in your textbook.

13.9 According to _____, long-term weight loss maintenance is dependent upon whether there is the perception of autonomous control or external control of the motivation to lose weight.
 a. This answer is incorrect because this theory does not address long-term weight loss maintenance specifically. Review page 514 in your textbook.
 b. This answer is incorrect because this theory does not address long-term weight loss maintenance specifically. Review page 514 in your textbook.
 c. For more information, see page 514 in your textbook.
 d. This answer is incorrect because this theory does not address long-term weight loss maintenance specifically. Review page 514 in your textbook.

13.10 In the Type A behavior pattern, there is a positive correlation between risk for heart risk and
 a. This answer is incorrect because emotional variability is not involved in this relationship. Review page 517 in your textbook.
 b. This answer is incorrect because affective threshold is not involved in this relationship. Review page 517 in your textbook.
 c. This answer is incorrect because physical activity is not involved in this relationship. Review page 517 in your textbook.
 d. For more information, see page 517 in your textbook.

13.11 One model that has been found useful for developing intervention strategies for groups of individuals thought to be at risk for HIV is
 a. This answer is incorrect because this model is not appropriate for individuals at risk for HIV. Review page 519 in your textbook.
 b. For more information, see page 519 in your textbook.
 c. This answer is incorrect because this model is not appropriate for individuals at risk for HIV. Review page 519 in your textbook.
 d. This answer is incorrect because this model is not appropriate for individuals at risk for HIV. Review page 519 in your textbook.

13.12 The most important factor contributing to longevity and good health seems to be
 a. This answer is incorrect because moderate consumption may actually be beneficial to certain individuals. Review page 521 in your textbook.
 b. For more information, see page 521 in your textbook.
 c. This answer is incorrect because such a diet may be detrimental. Review page 521 in your textbook.
 d. This answer is incorrect because such intake is detrimental to good health. Review page 521 in your textbook.

13.13　Which of the following is **not** listed as a factor that might contribute to an extended life span?
   a.　This answer is incorrect because it was one of the factors listed as potentially contributing to an extended lifespan. Review page 521 in your textbook.
   b.　This answer is incorrect because it was one of the factors listed as potentially contributing to an extended lifespan. Review page 521 in your textbook.
   c.　For more information, see page 521 in your textbook.
   d.　This answer is incorrect because it was one of the factors listed as potentially contributing to an extended lifespan. Review page 521 in your textbook.

13.14　Prevention strategies that are designed to increase early detection are called
   a.　This answer is incorrect because there is no such strategy category. Review page 521 in your textbook.
   b.　This answer is incorrect because there is not such strategy category. Review page 521 in your textbook.
   c.　This answer is incorrect because primary strategies are designed to reduce or eliminate preventable illness and injury. Review page 521 in your textbook.
   d.　For more information, see page 521 in your textbook.

13.15　If an individual replaces negative appraisals of stressors with positive appraisals, that individual has engaged in
   a.　This answer is incorrect because cognitive framing would involve how an individual asks a question about stress. Review page 527 in your textbook.
   b.　This answer is incorrect because cognitive enhancement would not be related to appraisal of stressors. Review page 527 in your textbook.
   c.　For more information, see page 527 in your textbook.
   d.　This answer is incorrect because cognitive confinement would not be related to appraisal of stressors. Review page 527 in your textbook.

13.16　The _____ of an individual involves the overall pattern of decisions and behaviors that determine health and quality of life.
   a.　For more information, see page 491 in your textbook.
   b.　This answer is incorrect because cognitive structure does not involve behaviors. Review page 491 in your textbook.
   c.　This answer is incorrect because a person's genetic makeup does not directly influence decisions. Review page 491 in your textbook.
   d.　This answer is incorrect because the experience of an individual is not defined in this particular way. Review page 491 in your textbook.

13.17　As a result of continued stress, you seem to catch every flu bug that comes around. Which stage of the general adaptation syndrome are you most likely to be experiencing?
   a.　This answer is incorrect because weakness is not a stage. Review page 495 in your textbook.
   b.　This answer is incorrect because the alarm stage gets you ready for immediate action. Review page 495 in your textbook.
   c.　This answer is incorrect because the resistance stage is a defensive stage to cope with the stressor. Review page 495 in your textbook.
   d.　For more information, see page 495 in your textbook.

13.18 Individuals who remain healthy even after prolonged exposure to high levels of stress are called
   a. For more information, see page 498 in your textbook.
   b. This answer is incorrect because resilient is not a trait concerned with stress. Review page 498 in your textbook.
   c. This answer is incorrect because adaptors adjust to the environment, regardless of the stress level. Review page 498 in your textbook.
   d. This answer is incorrect because innovators try to change the environment, even when there is not chance of success. Review page 498 in your textbook..

13.19 Annoying minor events of everyday life that cumulatively can affect psychological well-being are called
   a. This answer is incorrect because annoyances is not the correct name. Review page 498 in your textbook.
   b. For more information, see page 498 in your textbook.
   c. This answer is incorrect because stressors are general and could operate singly or in combination. Review page 498 in your textbook.
   d. This answer is incorrect because repeats is not a relevant name. Review page 498 in your textbook.

13.20 People who have general expectancies for poor outcomes in challenging situations are said to be
   a. This answer is incorrect because unrealistic is not an appropriate descriptor. Review page 502 in your textbook.
   b. This answer is incorrect because delusional is a term having to do with abnormal behavior. Review page 502 in your textbook.
   c. For more information, see page 502 in your textbook.
   d. This answer is incorrect because such a person may not be exhausted. Review page 502 in your textbook.

13.21 A coping strategy that involves a set of specific steps for identifying the stressor, choosing a method of stress reduction, implementing the method and evaluating its success is a(n) _____ strategy.
   a. This answer is incorrect because the phrase "external strategy" is not relevant. Review page 503 in your textbook.
   b. This answer is incorrect because the phrase "internal strategy" is not relevant. Review page 503 in your textbook.
   c. This answer is incorrect because defense-oriented strategy is not relevant. Review page 503 in your textbook.
   d. For more information, see page 503 in your textbook.

13.22 Lifestyle features that affect our chances of becoming ill are termed _____ factors.
   a. For more information, see page 509 in your textbook.
   b. This answer is incorrect because carcinogen factors have to do with cancer specifically. Review page 509 in your textbook.
   c. This answer is incorrect because punishment factors are not relevant nor descriptive. Review page 509 in your textbook.
   d. This answer is incorrect because individual factors are not relevant nor descriptive. Review page 509 in your textbook.

13.23   Which of the following is not likely to influence your decision to smoke?
- a.   This answer is incorrect because biological factors are factors that might influence you. Review page 511 in your textbook.
- b.   For more information, see page 511 in your textbook.
- c.   This answer is incorrect because psychological factors are factors that might influence you. Review page 511 in your textbook.
- d.   This answer is incorrect because cognitive factors are factors that might influence you. Review page 511 in your textbook.

13.24   The _____ personality type is characterized by a general tendency to cope with stress by keeping negative emotions to him or her self.
- a.   This answer is incorrect because Type A personality type involves cynical hostility. Review page 517 in your textbook.
- b.   For more information, see page 517 in your textbook.
- c.   This answer is incorrect because Type B personality type involves a lower level of activity. Review page 517 in your textbook.
- d.   This answer is incorrect because Type E does not exist. Review page 517 in your textbook.

13.25   Prevention strategies that are designed to increase early detection are called
- a.   This answer is incorrect because preliminary strategies are not one of the categories. Review page 524 in your textbook.
- b.   This answer is incorrect because there are no tertiary prevention strategies. Review page 524 in your textbook.
- c.   This answer is incorrect because primary prevention strategies involve reducing or eliminating the risk through education and other activities. Review page 524 in your textbook.
- d.   For more information, see page 524 in your textbook.

124

Chapter 13 - Practice Test Answers

Question	Answer
13.1	a
13.2	b
13.3	c
13.4	b
13.5	c
13.6	a
13.7	b
13.8	d
13.9	c
13.10	d
13.11	b
13.12	b
13.13	c
13.14	d
13.15	c
13.16	a
13.17	d
13.18	a
13.19	b
13.20	c
13.21	d
13.22	a
13.23	b
13.24	b
13.25	d

Chapter 14 - Practice Test

14.1   The beginnings of the medical view of mental disorders in France had the immediate effect of
   a.   removing the mentally ill from society in a form of guarantee.
   b.   blaming mental disorders on the actions of spirits or demons.
   c.   developing highly effective treatments using common herbal remedies.
   d.   drastically improving the living conditions in mental institutions.

14.2   One goal of the DSM-IV is to
   a.   organize disorders into categories on the basis of etiological evidence.
   b.   improve the reliability of diagnosis.
   c.   introduce a common terminology into the mental health field.
   d.   describe preventative measures.

14.3   Ralph is using the technique of _____ to observe an individual in a specific situation to see if there are any target behaviors causing distress for this individual.
   a.   behavior assessment
   b.   participant observation
   c.   social assessment
   d.   self-monitoring

14.4   According to the DSM-IV, if an individual has experienced five or more symptoms such as loss of appetite, disturbance of sleep, thinking difficulties, thoughts of death, and excessive guilt, that individual would be classified as having
   a.   a psychotic episode.
   b.   a major depressive episode.
   c.   a suicidal tendency.
   d.   a schizophrenic attack.

14.5   Which of the following has **not** been found to be a potential cause for depression?
   a.   genetic inheritance
   b.   learned helplessness
   c.   high levels of neurotransmitters
   d.   negative self-schemas

14.6   A person who is _____ is less likely to commit suicide.
   a.   a teenager
   b.   deeply depressed
   c.   an older person
   d.   slightly depressed

14.7   Someone with a social phobia exhibits extreme fear and avoidance of
   a.   situations that involve being observed by other individuals.
   b.   being alone or in public places that are hard to exit.
   c.   any small, confined space with no obvious way out.
   d.   any specific object or situation that is not really dangerous.

14.8   The disorder that involves anxieties that involve repetitive behaviors is called
   a.   obsessive-compulsive.
   b.   phobia.
   c.   panic.
   d.   generalized anxiety.

14.9 When a person appears to have two or more distinct personalities, that person is said
to have which disorder?
a. schizophrenic disorder.
b. somatoform disorder.
c. conversion disorder.
d. dissociative identity disorder.

14.10 Lisa is probably suffering from a _____ since she is blind but there are no underlying medical reasons
for her blindness.
a. phobic disorder
b. posttraumatic stress disorder
c. conversion disorder
d. schizophrenic attack

14.11 A person who cannot experience sexual arousal without an unusual or bizarre act occurring is said
to be suffering from a
a. paraphilia disorder.
b. phobic disorder.
c. sexual desire disorder.
d. dissociative disorder.

14.12 Ralph knows a person who is very suspicious and mistrustful, even to the extent of thinking that
everyone is out to get him or take advantage of him. The DSM-IV would classify this person
as suffering from a _____ personality disorder.
a. schizotypal
b. schizoid
c. paranoid
d. borderline

14.13 The most common perceptual distortions experienced by schizophrenics are _____ hallucinations.
a. visual
b. auditory
c. olfactory
d. gustatory

14.14 A schizophrenic who has delusions of grandeur and persecution claiming to be Emperor
Nero is most likely a _____ type.
a. disorganized
b. paranoid
c. catatonic
d. undifferentiated

14.15 One hypothesis concerning the cause of schizophrenia is that schizophrenics may have an abnormally
high level of
a. serotonin.
b. adrenal choline.
c. neurotoxin.
d. dopamine.

14.16 The earliest written description of mental disorders puts the cause of the maladies on
a. biological causes.
b. supernatural causes.
c. childhood trauma.
d. diseases.

14.17 Which of the following is **not** listed as one of the perspective that have to be considered with dealing with mental disorders?
   a. biological perspective
   b. cognitive perspective
   c. psychological perspective
   d. sociocultural perspective

14.18 When individuals are very fearful of gaining weight and fail to maintain a normal body weight, they have
   a. paraphilia nervosa.
   b. anorexia nervosa.
   c. bulimia nervosa.
   d. neologism nervosa.

14.19 Bipolar disorder and depressive disorders are considered to be _____ disorders.
   a. personality
   b. anxiety
   c. dissociative
   d. mood

14.20 The research by Beck suggests that the thinking of depressed people is characterized by what he calls the
   a. global thinking hypothesis.
   b. negative cognitive triad.
   c. restricted arrangement technique.
   d. "worst case scenario" process.

14.21 The risk of suicide is greatest for individuals with the mental disorder of
   a. depression.
   b. hypochondriasis.
   c. agoraphobia.
   d. dissociative disorders.

14.22 Dissociative amnesia is classified as a _____ disorder.
   a. dissociative
   b. schizophrenic
   c. somatoform
   d. personality

14.23 Fetishes, frotteurism, pedophilia, sexual sadism, and sexual masochism belong to the category of disorders called
   a. sexual dysfunction.
   b. sexual desire disorders.
   c. fugue.
   d. paraphilias.

14.24 Symptoms involving the presence of something that is not normally present, for example, hallucinations, are called
   a. transient symptoms.
   b. neutral symptoms.
   c. negative symptoms.
   d. positive symptoms.

128

14.25   The term that refers to the jumbled and meaningless speech patterns shown by schizophrenics
        who jump from one topic to the next with no organization is
        a.   delusion.
        b.   hallucination.
        c.   paraphilia.
        d.   verbal salad.

Chapter 14 - Practice Test Answer Justifications

14.1   The beginnings of the medical view of psychological disorders in France had the immediate effect of
   a.   This answer is incorrect because the mentally ill were already removed from society. Review page 534 in your textbook.
   b.   This answer is incorrect because such blame had already occurred in another model of mental illness. Review page 534 in your textbook.
   c.   This answer is incorrect because such treatments were not the result of the medical view in France. Review page 534 in your textbook.
   d.   For more information, see page 534 in your textbook.

14.2   One goal of the DSM-IV is to
   a.   This answer is incorrect because the DSM-IV avoids categories and uses five axes for description. Review page 538 in your textbook.
   b.   For more information, see page 538 in your textbook.
   c.   This answer is incorrect because common terminology is not a goal, and such a goal might be a hindrance to reliable diagnosis. Review page 538 in your textbook.
   d.   This answer is incorrect because preventive measures were definitely not a goal, only description of disorders. Review page 538 in your textbook.

14.3   Ralph is using the technique of _____ to observe an individual in a specific situation to see if there are any target behaviors causing distress for this individual.
   a.   For more information, see page 541 in your textbook.
   b.   This answer is incorrect because the person doing the observation would participate in the activity. Review page 541 in your textbook.
   c.   This answer is incorrect because social assessment would involve assessing the social setting, not the individual's behavior. Review page 541 in your textbook.
   d.   This answer is incorrect because self-monitoring would involve the individual recording behavior, not an observer. Review page 541 in your textbook.

14.4   According to the DSM-IV, if an individual has experienced five or more symptoms such as loss of appetite, disturbance of sleep, thinking difficulties, thoughts of death, and excessive guilt, that individual is classified as having
   a.   This answer is incorrect because psychotic is not the term used to describe these symptoms. Review page 549 in your textbook.
   b.   For more information, see page 549 in your textbook.
   c.   This answer is incorrect because suicide usually does not occur with major depressed individuals. Review page 549 in your textbook.
   d.   This answer is incorrect because such behaviors are not characteristic of schizophrenia. Review page 549 in your textbook.

14.5   Which of the following has **not** been found to be a potential cause for depression?
   a.   This answer is incorrect because genetic inheritance has been found to play a role in depression. Review page 551 in your textbook.
   b.   This answer is incorrect because learned helplessness has been found to play a role in depression. Review page 551 in your textbook.
   c.   For more information, see page 551 in your textbook.
   d.   This answer is incorrect because faulty cognitive sets have been found to play a role in depression. Review page 551 in your textbook.

14.6 A person who is _____ is less likely to commit suicide.
   a. This answer is incorrect because the suicide rate for teenagers is on the rise. Review page 551 in your textbook.
   b. This answer is incorrect because being deeply depressed may result in a lack of energy to achieve real change. Review page 551 in your textbook.
   c. This answer is incorrect because the suicide rate is the highest for this group. Review page 551 in your textbook.
   d. For more information, see page 551 in your textbook.

14.7 Someone with a social phobia exhibits extreme fear and avoidance of
   a. For more information, see page 554 in your textbook.
   b. This answer is incorrect because there would be no one present to evaluate this individual. Review page 554 in your textbook.
   c. This answer is incorrect because this situation would describe a phobia of small, enclosed spaces. Review page 554 in your textbook.
   d. This answer is incorrect because this is a general description of a phobia. Review page 554 in your textbook.

14.8 The disorder that involves anxieties that involve repetitive behaviors is called
   a. For more information, see page 556 in your textbook.
   b. This answer is incorrect because a phobia is a fear of something that is not really dangerous. Review page 556 in your textbook.
   c. This answer is incorrect because a panic disorder is a generalized fear and does not involve repetition. Review page 556 in your textbook.
   d. This answer is incorrect because generalized anxiety does not involve repetitive behaviors. Review page 556 in your textbook.

14.9 When a person appears to have two or more distinct personalities, that person is said to have which disorder?
   a. This answer is incorrect because schizophrenia does not involve two separate personalities. Review page 558 in your textbook.
   b. This answer is incorrect because a somatoform disorder does not involve two separate personalities. Review page 558 in your textbook.
   c. This answer is incorrect because a conversion disorder involves a physical disorder not two separate personalities. Review page 558 in your textbook.
   d. For more information, see page 558 in your textbook.

14.10 Lisa is probably suffering from a _____ since she is blind but there are no underlying medical reasons for her blindness.
   a. This answer is incorrect because a phobia involves a fear of something that is not dangerous. Review page 560 in your textbook.
   b. This answer is incorrect because this disorder involves generalized reaction to a stressful situation that has already occurred. Review page 560 in your textbook.
   c. For more information, see page 560 in your textbook.
   d. This answer is incorrect because schizophrenia is a much more generalized and severe disorder. Review page 560 in your textbook.

14.11 A person who cannot experience sexual arousal without an unusual or bizarre act occurring is said to be suffering from a
  a. For more information, see page 562 in your textbook.
  b. This answer is incorrect because a phobia involves excessive fear of something. Review page 562 in your textbook.
  c. This answer is incorrect because this disorder involves a lack of interest or actual aversion to sexual activity. Review page 562 in your textbook.
  d. This answer is incorrect because this disorder involves the loss of memory and depersonalization. Review page 562 in your textbook.

14.12 Ralph knows a person who is very suspicious and mistrustful, even to the extent of thinking that everyone is out to get him or take advantage of him. The DSM-IV would classify this person as suffering from a _____ personality disorder.
  a. This answer is incorrect because a schizotypal disorder involves social isolation and avoidance of close relationships. Review page 563 in your textbook.
  b. This answer is incorrect because a schizoid personality involves little emotion and lack basic social skills. Review page 563 in your textbook.
  c. For more information, see page 563 in your textbook.
  d. This answer is incorrect because a borderline personality involves instability in their interpersonal relationships. Review page 563 in your textbook.

14.13 The most common perceptual distortions experienced by schizophrenics are _____ hallucinations.
  a. This answer is incorrect because visual are not as common as auditory hallucinations. Review page 567 in your textbook.
  b. For more information, see page 567 in your textbook.
  c. This answer is incorrect because olfactory hallucinations are rare in schizophrenics. Review page 567 in your textbook.
  d. This answer is incorrect because gustatory hallucinations are rare in schizophrenics. Review page 567 in your textbook.

14.14 A schizophrenic who has delusions of grandeur and persecution (e.g., claiming to be Emperor Nero who everyone is out to kill) is most likely a _____ type.
  a. This answer is incorrect because a disorganized schizophrenia would have poorly developed delusions. Review page 569 in your textbook.
  b. For more information, see page 569 in your textbook.
  c. This answer is incorrect because a catatonic schizophrenia would have unusual motor activity. Review page 569 in your textbook.
  d. This answer is incorrect because an undifferentiated schizophrenic would have many symptoms. Review page 569 in your textbook.

14.15 One hypothesis concerning the cause of schizophrenia is that schizophrenics may have an abnormally high level of
  a. This answer is incorrect because this biochemical is not directly related to schizophrenia. Review page 570 in your textbook.
  b. This answer is incorrect because this biochemical is not directly related to schizophrenia. Review page 570 in your textbook.
  c. This answer is incorrect because this biochemical is not directly related to schizophrenia. Review page 570 in your textbook.
  d. For more information, see page 570 in your textbook.

132

14.16   The earliest written description of mental disorders puts the cause of the maladies on
    a. This answer is incorrect because the level of understanding of biological causes was quite low. Review page 533 in your textbook.
    b. For more information, see page 533 in your textbook.
    c. This answer is incorrect because childhood trauma was not even considered. Review page 533 in your textbook.
    d. This answer is incorrect because diseases were not yet understood. Review page 533 in your textbook.

14.17   Which of the following is **not** listed as one of the perspective that have to be considered with dealing with mental disorders?
    a. This answer is incorrect because biological perspective was one of the perspectives listed. Review page 535 in your textbook.
    b. For more information, see page 535 in your textbook.
    c. This answer is incorrect because psychological perspective was one of the perspectives listed. Review page 535 in your textbook.
    d. This answer is incorrect because sociocultural perspective was one of the perspectives listed. Review page 535 in your textbook.

14.18   When individuals are very fearful of gaining weight and fail to maintain a normal body weight, they have
    a. This answer is incorrect because paraphilia nervosa is not a disorder. Review page 545 in your textbook.
    b. For more information, see page 545 in your textbook.
    c. This answer is incorrect because bulimia nervosa involves purging. Review page 545 in your textbook.
    d. This answer is incorrect because neologism nervosa is not a disorder. Review page 545 in your textbook.

14.19   Bipolar disorder and depressive disorders are considered to be _____ disorders.
    a. This answer is incorrect because personality disorders include other disorders. Review page 549 in your textbook.
    b. This answer is incorrect because anxiety disorders include other disorders. Review page 549 in your textbook.
    c. This answer is incorrect because dissociative disorders include other disorders. Review page 549 in your textbook.
    d. For more information, see page 549 in your textbook.

14.20   The research by Beck suggests that the thinking of depressed people is characterized by what he calls the
    a. This answer is incorrect because the global thinking hypothesis would involve very primitive thinking, without interactions. Review page 551 in your textbook.
    b. For more information, see page 551 in your textbook.
    c. This answer is incorrect because the restricted arrangement technique does not exist. Review page 551 in your textbook.
    d. This answer is incorrect because the "worst case scenario" process does not involve depressed people exclusively. Review page 551 in your textbook.

14.21   The risk of suicide is greatest for individuals with the mental disorder of
   a.   For more information, see page 551 in your textbook.
   b.   This answer is incorrect because hypochondriasis would lead to more visits to the hospital. Review page 551 in your textbook.
   c.   This answer is incorrect because agoraphobia does not necessarily include depression. Review page 551 in your textbook.
   d.   This answer is incorrect because dissociative disorders do not necessarily involve depression. Review page 551 in your textbook.

14.22   Dissociative amnesia is classified as a _____ disorder.
   a.   For more information, see page 558 in your textbook.
   b.   This answer is incorrect because schizophrenic disorders are much more severe. Review page 558 in your textbook.
   c.   This answer is incorrect because somatoform disorders don't involve amnesia. Review page 558 in your textbook.
   d.   This answer is incorrect because personality disorders usually do not involve amnesia. Review page 558 in your textbook.

14.23   Fetishes, frotteurism, pedophilia, sexual sadism, and sexual masochism belong to the category of disorders called
   a.   This answer is incorrect because sexual dysfunction involves the inability to perform sexually. Review page 562 in your textbook.
   b.   This answer is incorrect because sexual desire disorders involve a decrease in sexual desire. Review page 562 in your textbook.
   c.   This answer is incorrect because a fugue is a dissociative disorder, not a sexual disorder. Review page 562 in your textbook.
   d.   For more information, see page 562 in your textbook.

14.24   Symptoms involving the presence of something that is not normally present, for example, hallucinations, are called
   a.   This answer is incorrect because transient symptoms are not relevant. Review page 567 in your textbook.
   b.   This answer is incorrect because neutral symptoms are not relevant. Review page 567 in your textbook.
   c.   This answer is incorrect because negative symptoms involve the reduction of normal functions. Review page 567 in your textbook.
   d.   For more information, see page 567 in your textbook.

14.25   The term that refers to the jumbled and meaningless speech patterns shown by schizophrenics who jump from one topic to the next with no organization is
   a.   This answer is incorrect because delusions involve cognitive processes. Review page 568 in your textbook.
   b.   This answer is incorrect because hallucinations involve hearing or seeing things. Review page 568 in your textbook.
   c.   This answer is incorrect because paraphilia is a sexual disorder. Review page 568 in your textbook.
   d.   For more information, see page 568 in your textbook.

Chapter 14 - Practice Test Answers

Question	Answer
14.1	d
14.2	b
14.3	a
14.4	b
14.5	c
14.6	d
14.7	a
14.8	a
14.9	d
14.10	c
14.11	a
14.12	c
14.13	b
14.14	b
14.15	d
14.16	b
14.17	b
14.18	b
14.19	d
14.20	b
14.21	a
14.22	a
14.23	d
14.24	d
14.25	d

Chapter 15 - Practice Test

15.1   According to Freud, mental disorders stem from conflicts between
   a.   ego versus superego.
   b.   id versus ego versus superego.
   c.   conscious versus preconscious.
   d.   sexual drives versus libidinal drives.

15.2   The types of therapy that helps clients become more truly themselves are called
   a.   behavioral therapies.
   b.   psychoanalytic therapies
   c.   phenomenological/experiential therapies.
   d.   cognitive therapies

15.3   A humanistic therapy that focuses on helping individuals reclaim lost parts of their being in order to become whole is referred to as
   a.   Gestalt therapy.
   b.   client-centered therapy
   c.   person-centered therapy
   d.   rational-emotive therapy

15.4   Therapies based on the principles of learning are
   a.   person-centered therapies.
   b.   psychoanalytic therapies.
   c.   Gestalt therapies.
   d.   behavioral therapies.

15.5   In _____, an individual is taught the basic social skills that he or she might be lacking.
   a.   modeling training
   b.   person-centered training
   b.   assertiveness training
   d.   desensitization training

15.6   Lisa was using the process of _____ when she failed a test and thought that her whole academic career was going to end.
   a.   irrational thinking
   b.   discrimination
   c.   transference
   d.   resistance

15.7   According to Beck's cognitive therapy, depression is caused by
   a.   a discrepancy between the self-concept and reality.
   b.   unconscious conflicts created in early childhood.
   c.   a chemical imbalance in the cerebral cortex.
   d.   distorted thoughts that make a person feel worthless.

15.8   Which of these is **not** a form of group therapy?
   a.   Assertiveness training
   b.   Psychodrama
   c.   Social skills training
   d.   Cognitive behavior training

15.9 Problems of _____ are the number one cause of difficulties in marriages.
a. communication
b. sex
c. money
d. in-laws

15.10 The family therapist with whom Ralph is working uses _____, which focuses on instituting specific, well-defined changes within the family.
a. affective framing therapy
b. cognitive restructuring therapy
c. psychoanalytic procedure therapy
d. problem-solving therapy

15.11 One possible side effect of the extended use of antipsychotic drugs is _____, the loss of motor control, especially in the face.
a. antithetic disorder
b. epiglottis distortion
c. tardive dyskinesia
d. phalanges dysfunction

15.12 Most research on the effectiveness of psychotherapy supports which of these conclusions?
a. People who receive no treatment improve most.
b. People who receive psychotherapy improve most.
c. Psychotherapy is just as effective as no treatment.
d. No general conclusions can be drawn from the research.

15.13 All forms of psychotherapy have a common core of features that includes
a. a belief in the importance of the unconscious.
b. an explanation for the client's problems.
c. an agreement on the causes of disorders.
d. a desire to aid the client's personal growth.

15.14 Primary prevention refers to programs designed to
a. assess the psychological damage of an event.
b. detect mental disorders early.
c. prevent mental disorders from occurring.
d. ease the pain of mental disorders.

15.15 Which of the following is **not** suggested as a way of choosing a therapist?
a. matching the therapist with same-sex clients
b. checking the therapist's credentials
c. matching the therapist's specialization with the type of problem suffered by the client
d. matching the therapist's preferred techniques of therapy with those with which the client feels most comfortable

15.16 According to Freud, the release of emotion obtained as a result of understanding unconscious conflicts is called
a. transference.
b. resistance.
c. abreaction.
d. relief.

15.17 A form of therapy that tries to help people understand themselves and the world from their own person, unique perspectives, without the therapist telling the client what to do or what it means, is
a. behavioral therapy.
b. psychoanalysis.
c. somatic therapy.
d. client-centered therapy.

15.18 If asked to perform the empty-chair exercise -- moving back and forth between two chairs playing themselves in one chair and the role of some other person in another chair -- you are probably seeing which of the following therapists?
a. behavioral
b. client-centered
c. gestalt
d. cognitive

15.19 Which of the following clinical procedures are based, in part, on classical conditioning?
a. transference
b. systematic desensitization
c. two-chair technique
d. token economy

15.20 Having children who show high levels of aggressive behavior watch films of children behaving in a nonaggressive manner is an attempt to change their behavior through
a. classical conditioning.
b. transference.
c. shaping.
d. modeling.

15.21 Recent research has indicated that cognitive therapies may be highly effective in treating _____.
a. schizophrenia.
b. phobias.
c. depression.
d. anxiety disorders.

15.22 Drugs that are prescribed for the purpose of treating mental disorders are called
a. recreational drugs.
b. psychoactive drugs.
c. psychological drugs.
d. behavioral drugs.

15.23 Lithium is used to treat
a. bipolar disorders.
b. schizophrenia.
c. obsessive-compulsive disorders.
d. paranoid delusions.

15.24 Which of the following is **not** one of the features held in common by the different therapies?
a. therapeutic alliance
b. psychodrama
c. special kind of setting
d. suggestion of specific actions in order to cope with problems

15.25   Preventing mental disorders from developing refers to _____ prevention.
   a.   primary
   b.   secondary
   c.   tertiary
   d.   milieu

Chapter 15 - Practice Test Answer Justifications

15.1 According to Freud, psychological disorders stem from conflicts between
   a. This answer is incorrect because the id is usually involved in conflict. Review page 580 in your textbook.
   b. For more information, see page 580 in your textbook.
   c. This answer is incorrect because these concepts are not capable of conflict. Review page 580 in your textbook.
   d. This answer is incorrect because these two drives are essentially the same. Review page 580 in your textbook.

15.2 The types of therapy that helps clients become more truly themselves are called
   a. This answer is incorrect because behavioral therapies involve reinforcement and punishment. Review page 582 in your textbook.
   b. This answer is incorrect because psychoanalytic therapies involve resolving conflicts of id, ego, and superego. Review page 582 in your textbook.
   c. For more information, see page 582 in your textbook.
   d. This answer is incorrect because cognitive therapies involve how individuals think about situations. Review page 582 in your textbook.

15.3 A humanistic therapy that focuses on helping individuals reclaim lost parts of their being in order to become whole is referred to as
   a. For more information, see page 583 in your textbook.
   b. This answer is incorrect because this type of therapy focuses on creating a climate in which the client feels accepted. Review page 583 in your textbook.
   c. This answer is incorrect because this type of therapy is another name for client-centered therapy and focuses on creating a climate in which the client feels accepted. Review page 583 in your textbook.
   d. This answer is incorrect because this therapy involves cognitive processes. Review page 583 in your textbook.

15.4 Therapies based on the principles of learning are
   a. This answer is incorrect because these types of therapies create an environment in which the client feels accepted. Review page 584 in your textbook.
   b. This answer is incorrect because these therapies involve conflict between id, ego, and superego. Review page 584 in your textbook.
   c. This answer is incorrect because these therapies involve processes in which the client becomes "whole" again. Review page 584 in your textbook.
   d. For more information, see page 584 in your textbook.

15.5 In _____, an individual is taught the basic social skills that he or she might be lacking.
   a. For more information, see page 586 in your textbook.
   b. This answer is incorrect because this type of training creates a climate in which the client feels accepted. Review page 586 in your textbook.
   c. This answer is incorrect because assertiveness training is a modeling method used to help clients express their feelings and desires more effectively. Review page 586 in your textbook.
   d. This answer is incorrect because desensitization training involves systematic exposure to things one fears. Review page 586 in your textbook.

15.6   Lisa was using the process of _____ when she failed a test and thought that her whole academic career was going to end.
  a.   For more information, see page 587 in your textbook.
  b.   This answer is incorrect because discrimination is not involved in this situation. Review page 587 in your textbook.
  c.   This answer is incorrect because transference is a psychoanalytic process. Review page 587 in your textbook.
  d.   This answer is incorrect because resistance is a psychoanalytic process. Review page 587 in your textbook.

15.7   According to Beck's cognitive therapy, depression is caused by
  a.   This answer is incorrect because the self-concept is not a part of cognitive therapy. Review page 588 in your textbook.
  b.   This answer is incorrect because unconscious conflicts are not a part of cognitive therapy. Review page 588 in your textbook.
  c.   This answer is incorrect because chemical balance is not a part of cognitive therapy. Review page 588 in your textbook.
  d.   For more information, see page 588 in your textbook.

15.8   Which of these is **not** a form of group therapy?
  a.   This answer is incorrect because assertiveness training can be practiced in a group therapy situation. Review page 590 in your textbook.
  b.   This answer is incorrect because psychodrama can be practiced in a group therapy situation. Review page 590 in your textbook.
  c.   This answer is incorrect because social skills training can be practiced in a group therapy situation. Review page 590 in your textbook.
  d.   For more information, see page 590 in your textbook.

15.9   Problems of _____ are the number one cause of difficulties in marriages.
  a.   For more information, see page 592 in your textbook.
  b.   This answer is incorrect because even though sex is important in a marriage, it is a distant second as a cause of difficulty in marriage. Review page 592 in your textbook.
  c.   This answer is incorrect because financial issues were last on the list of causes of difficulties. Review page 592 in your textbook.
  d.   This answer is incorrect because in-laws were not the number one cause of difficulties in a marriage. Review page 592 in your textbook.

15.10 The family therapist with whom Ralph is working uses _____, which focuses on instituting specific, well-defined changes within the family.
  a.   This answer is incorrect because this type of therapy does not focus on specific changes. Review page 595 in your textbook.
  b.   This answer is incorrect because this type of therapy does not focus on specific changes. Review page 595 in your textbook.
  c.   This answer is incorrect because this type of therapy involves conflict of id, ego, and superego. Review page 595 in your textbook.
  d.   For more information, see page 595 in your textbook.

15.11   One possible side effect of the extended use of antipsychotic drugs is _____, the loss of motor control, especially in the face.
   a.   This answer is incorrect because this is not a side effect of antipsychotic drugs. Review page 598 in your textbook.
   b.   This answer is incorrect because the epiglottis is in the back of the mouth and does not distort. Review page 598 in your textbook.
   c.   For more information, see page 598 in your textbook.
   d.   This answer is incorrect because phalanges are fingers and toes and they are not affected by antipsychotic drugs. Review page 598 in your textbook.

15.12   Most research on the effectiveness of psychotherapy supports which of these conclusions?
   a.   This answer is incorrect because this relationship is not supported by the data. Review page 605 in your textbook.
   b.   For more information, see page 605 in your textbook.
   c.   This answer is incorrect because this finding was supported by an early study, but not supported by later studies. Review page 605 in your textbook.
   d.   This answer is incorrect because a general conclusion can be drawn from the data. Review page 605 in your textbook.

15.13   All forms of psychotherapy have a common core of features that includes
   a.   This answer is incorrect because not all psychotherapies have the unconscious as a foundation for therapy. Review page 606 in your textbook.
   b.   For more information, see page 606 in your textbook.
   c.   This answer is incorrect because there usually is no agreement on the cause. Review page 606 in your textbook.
   d.   This answer is incorrect because this desire is usually part of humanistic therapies. Review page 606 in your textbook.

15.14   Primary prevention refers to programs designed to
   a.   This answer is incorrect because primary prevention is not involved in assessment after an event has occurred. Review page 608 in your textbook.
   b.   This answer is incorrect because early detection is the realm of secondary prevention. Review page 608 in your textbook.
   c.   For more information, see page 608 in your textbook.
   d.   This answer is incorrect because primary prevention is not involved in easing pain, but prevention. Review page 608 in your textbook.

15.15   Which of the following is **not** suggested as a way of choosing a therapist?
   a.   For more information, see page 613 in your textbook.
   b.   This answer is incorrect because checking credentials is listed as one of the considerations of choosing a therapist. Review page 613 in your textbook.
   c.   This answer is incorrect because matching specialization and problem is listed as one of the considerations of choosing a therapist. Review page 613 in your textbook.
   d.   This answer is incorrect because exaggerated claims is listed as one of the considerations of choosing a therapist. Review page 613 in your textbook.

15.16 According to Freud, the release of emotion obtained as a result of understanding unconscious conflicts is called
  a. This answer is incorrect because transference involves intense feelings of love or hate toward the therapist. Review page 580 in your textbook.
  b. This answer is incorrect because resistance involves a patient's refusal to reveal everything to the therapist. Review page 580 in your textbook.
  c. For more information, see page 580 in your textbook.
  d. This answer is incorrect because relief is not relevant to unconscious conflicts. Review page 580 in your textbook.

15.17 A form of therapy that tries to help people understand themselves and the world from their own person, unique perspectives, without the therapist telling the client what to do or what it means, is
  a. This answer is incorrect because behavioral therapy doesn't involve understanding of self. Review page 582 in your textbook.
  b. This answer is incorrect because psychoanalysis is involved in directing the client's behavior and decisions. Review page 582 in your textbook.
  c. This answer is incorrect because somatic therapy deals with the skin senses and the environment. Review page 582 in your textbook.
  d. For more information, see page 582 in your textbook.

15.18 If asked to perform the empty-chair exercise -- moving back and forth between two chairs playing themselves in one chair and the role of some other person in another chair -- you are probably seeing which of the following therapists?
  a. This answer is incorrect because behavioral therapists would not use this technique. Review page 583 in your textbook.
  b. This answer is incorrect because client-centered therapists would not use such role playing. Review page 583 in your textbook.
  c. For more information, see page 583 in your textbook.
  d. This answer is incorrect because cognitive therapists would involve how a client understands the environment. Review page 583 in your textbook.

15.19 Which of the following clinical procedures are based, in part, on classical conditioning?
  a. This answer is incorrect because transference is psychoanalytic oriented. Review page 584 in your textbook.
  b. For more information, see page 584 in your textbook.
  c. This answer is incorrect because the two-chair technique is Gestalt therapy oriented. Review page 584 in your textbook.
  d. This answer is incorrect because token economy is part of behavior oriented therapy. Review page 584 in your textbook.

15.20 Having children who show high levels of aggressive behavior watch films of children behaving in a nonaggressive manner is an attempt to change their behavior through
  a. This answer is incorrect because classical conditioning would pair the aggression with some stimulus. Review page 586 in your textbook.
  b. This answer is incorrect because transference involves a client and therapist relationship. Review page 586 in your textbook.
  c. This answer is incorrect because shaping is a technique that when used with reinforcement can change behavior. Review page 586 in your textbook.
  d. For more information, see page 586 in your textbook.

15.21 Recent research has indicated that cognitive therapies may be highly effective in treating _____.
   a. This answer is incorrect because such therapies do not work well with schizophrenia. Review page 588 in your textbook.
   b. This answer is incorrect because phobias are more effectively treated with some form of behavior therapy, probably classical conditioning. Review page 588 in your textbook.
   c. For more information, see page 588 in your textbook.
   d. This answer is incorrect because anxiety disorders are more effectively treated with behavior therapies. Review page 588 in your textbook.

15.22 Drugs that are prescribed for the purpose of treating mental disorders are called
   a. This answer is incorrect because recreational drugs are usually not used for treatment. Review page 597 in your textbook.
   b. For more information, see page 597 in your textbook.
   c. This answer is incorrect because psychological drugs are not relevant to this question. Review page 597 in your textbook.
   d. This answer is incorrect because there is no class of behavioral drugs. Review page 597 in your textbook.

15.23 Lithium is used to treat
   a. For more information, see page 599 in your textbook.
   b. This answer is incorrect because Lithium is not used to treat schizophrenia. Review page 599 in your textbook.
   c. This answer is incorrect because Lithium is not used to treat obsessive-compulsive disorders. Review page 599 in your textbook.
   d. This answer is incorrect because Lithium is not used to treat paranoid delusions. Review page 599 in your textbook.

15.24 Which of the following is **not** one of the features held in common by the different therapies?
   a. This answer is incorrect because therapeutic alliance is one of the features held in common. Review page 606 in your textbook.
   b. For more information, see page 606 in your textbook.
   c. This answer is incorrect because special kind of setting is one of the features held in common. Review page 606 in your textbook.
   d. This answer is incorrect because suggestion of specific actions in order to cope with problems is one of the features held in common. Review page 606 in your textbook.

15.25 Preventing mental disorders from developing refers to _____ prevention.
   a. For more information, see page 608 in your textbook.
   b. This answer is incorrect because secondary prevention involves efforts of early detection of mental disorders. Review page 608 in your textbook.
   c. This answer is incorrect because tertiary prevention involves efforts to minimize long-term harm done by mental disorders. Review page 608 in your textbook.
   d. This answer is incorrect because milieu prevention does not exist. Review page 608 in your textbook.

Chapter 15 - Practice Test Answers

Question	Answer
15.1	b
15.2	c
15.3	a
15.4	d
15.5	a
15.6	a
15.7	d
15.8	d
15.9	a
15.10	d
15.11	c
15.12	b
15.13	b
15.14	c
15.15	a
15.16	c
15.17	d
15.18	c
15.19	b
15.20	d
15.21	c
15.22	b
15.23	a
15.24	b
15.25	a

Chapter 16 - Practice Test

16.1   According to one approach (Kelley), attribution is influenced primarily by
   a.   cognitive, emotional, and behavioral aspects.
   b.   stimuli, behaviors, and outcomes.
   c.   consensus, consistency, and distinctiveness.
   d.   compliance, conformity, and obedience.

16.2   Our strong tendency to explain others' behavior in terms of internal causes rather than external causes is called the
   a.   representative heuristic.
   b.   self-serving bias.
   c.   counterfactual thinking effect.
   d.   correspondence bias.

16.3   The tendency to take credit for positive behaviors or outcomes by attributing them to internal causes but to blame negative outcomes on external causes is called the
   a.   fundamental attribution error.
   b.   self-serving bias.
   c.   correspondence bias.
   d.   social contagion effect.

16.4   By bringing up alternative events and outcomes to an attempt to evaluate an unusual event, a person is engaging in
   a.   social construction activities.
   b.   peripheral route processing.
   c.   counterfactual thinking.
   d.   false consensus processes.

16.5   Attitudes are composed of three dimensions, which are
   a.   conscious, unconscious, and preconscious.
   b.   cognitive, affective, and behavioral.
   c.   internal, external, and conditional.
   d.   primary, secondary, and tertiary.

16.6   An individual who is _____ is more likely to be susceptible to persuasion.
   a.   elderly
   b.   competent
   c.   attractive
   d.   distracted

16.7   According to the elaboration likelihood model of persuasion, we are more likely to use the central route when
   a.   dealing with very important issues.
   b.   dealing with issues of little importance.
   c.   the issue is not personally relevant.
   d.   we can't invest much mental effort.

16.8   A technique for changing attitudes in which individuals are somehow induced to state positions different from their actual view is called
   a.   diffusion of responsibility.
   b.   induced compliance.
   c.   false consensus.
   d.   impression management.

16.9 Cognitive dissonance is produced when we
   a. are persuaded to change our minds about something.
   b. discover we hold two contradictory attitudes.
   c. make decisions based on too little information.
   d. find ourselves sexually attracted to someone.

16.10 The idea that prejudice stems from economic competition among social groups is a central proposal of:
   a. group polarization theory.
   b. social categorization theory.
   c. social learning theory.
   d. realistic conflict theory

16.11 A _____ is a cognitive framework that suggests that all members of a specific social group have the same characteristics.
   a. Gestalt
   b. contagion
   c. stereotype
   d. discrimination

16.12 Lisa has engaged in _____ when, to be accepted into the group, she wears a skirt to class, rather than the jeans she usually wears.
   a. contagion
   b. obedience
   c. compliance
   d. conformity

16.13 The foot-in-the-door technique is effective because of the pressure on individuals to
   a. behave consistently.
   b. behave rationally.
   c. behave competently.
   d. behave emotionally.

16.14 A compliance tactic in which individuals try to create the image that they are very popular or very much in demand is called
   a. ingratiation.
   b. reciprocity.
   c. playing hard to get.
   d. self-enhancing tactic.

6.15 This type of love emphasizes feelings of strong attraction and sexual desire toward another person.
   a. passionate love
   b. companionate love
   c. romantic love
   d. responsible love

16.16 The branch of psychology that investigates all aspects of social thought and social behavior is
   a. cognitive psychology.
   b. social psychology.
   c. attribution psychology.
   d. dissonance psychology.

16.17 You don't put much faith in the movie reviews in the paper, but when everyone you talk to agrees that the picture is terrific you decide to see it. The factor that convinced you is
a. compliance.
b. consistency.
c. distinctiveness.
d. consensus.

16.18 The correspondence bias is the tendency to explain the behavior of others in terms of _____ causes.
a. internal
b. external
c. stable
d. unstable

16.19 When we wish to make a decision quickly based on information that is already available using minimum effort, we will generally use
a. heuristics.
b. dissonance.
c. consensus.
d. recategorization.

16.20 The process of _____ involves one or more individuals attempting to alter the attitudes of one or more other individuals.
a. therapy
b. contagion
c. persuasion
d. development

16.21 According to the elaboration likelihood model, little cognitive activity is performed and attitude change involves a seemingly automatic response to persuasion cues through the
a. transient route.
b. diffusion route.
c. central route.
d. peripheral route.

16.22 According to cognitive dissonance theory, which of the following conditions is most likely to produce the greatest attitude change when asked to say something we do not believe to be true?
a. large reward
b. medium reward
c. small reward
d. no reward

16.23 Pressures toward thinking or acting like most other persons refers to
a. obedience.
b. deindividualization.
c. prosocial behavior.
d. conformity.

16.24 A form of social influence in which individuals attempt to influence others through direct requests is called
   a. conformity.
   b. compliance.
   c. obedience.
   d. consensus.

16.25 Which of the following is not a factor related to troubled marital relationships?
   a. jealousy
   b. boredom
   c. dissimilarities
   d. reciprocity

Chapter 16 - Practice Test Answer Jusifications

16.1   According to one approach (Kelley), attribution is influenced primarily by
   a.   This answer is incorrect because these aspects are too general and don't address attribution specifically. Review page 619 in your textbook.
   b.   This answer is incorrect because these aspects are not related to attribution specifically. Review page 619 in your textbook.
   c.   For more information, see page 619 in your textbook.
   d.   This answer is incorrect because these three are social influence tactics. Review page 619 in your textbook.

16.2   Our strong tendency to explain others' behavior in terms of internal causes rather than external causes is called the
   a.   This answer is incorrect because this heuristic involves recalling those features or individuals that are most representative of a category. Review page 621 in your textbook.
   b.   This answer is incorrect because self-serving bias involves attributing cause to internal factors for our own successes and to external factors for our own failures. Review page 621 in your textbook.
   c.   This answer is incorrect because this effect involves explaining behavior in terms of "what might have been." Review page 621 in your textbook.
   d.   For more information, see page 621 in your textbook.

16.3   The tendency to take credit for positive behaviors or outcomes by attributing them to internal causes but to blame negative outcomes on external causes is called the
   a.   This answer is incorrect because this errors is also called correspondence bias and involves explaining others' behavior in terms of internal causes. Review page 621 in your textbook.
   b.   For more information, see page 621 in your textbook.
   c.   This answer is incorrect because this bias involves explaining others' behavior in terms of internal causes. Review page 621 in your textbook.
   d.   This answer is incorrect because this effect involves the spreading of an effect to other individuals. Review page 621 in your textbook.

16.4   By bringing up alternative events and outcomes to an attempt to evaluate an unusual event, a person is engaging in
   a.   This answer is incorrect because these activities do not involve alternative outcomes for an unusual event. Review page 626 in your textbook.
   b.   This answer is incorrect because such processing involves short-term attitude change. Review page 626 in your textbook.
   c.   For more information, see page 626 in your textbook.
   d.   This answer is incorrect because these processes involve assuming that others agree with us to a greater extent than is true. Review page 626 in your textbook.

16.5   Attitudes are composed of three components, which are
   a.   This answer is incorrect because these components are part of psychoanalytic theory. Review page 628 in your textbook.
   b.   For more information, see page 628 in your textbook.
   c.   This answer is incorrect because these components are not related to attitudes. Review page 628 in your textbook.
   d.   This answer is incorrect because these components are related to mental disorder prevention and many other things, but not attitudes. Review page 628 in your textbook.

16.6   An individual who is _____ is more likely to be susceptible to persuasion.
   a.   This answer is incorrect because age of a person is not directly related to persuasion. Review page 629 in your textbook.
   b.   This answer is incorrect because competency is not directly related to persuasion. Review page 629 in your textbook.
   c.   This answer is incorrect because attractiveness is not directly related to persuasion. Review page 629 in your textbook.
   d.   For more information, see page 629 in your textbook.

16.7   According to the elaboration likelihood model of persuasion, we are more likely to use the central route to process information when
   a.   For more information, see page 630 in your textbook.
   b.   This answer is incorrect because in this situation we would use peripheral route processing. Review page 630 in your textbook.
   c.   This answer is incorrect because in this situation we would use peripheral route processing. Review page 630 in your textbook.
   d.   This answer is incorrect because in this situation we would use peripheral route processing. Review page 630 in your textbook.

16.8   A technique for changing attitudes in which individuals are somehow compelled to state positions different from their actual view is called
   a.   This answer is incorrect because diffusion of responsibility involves spreading responsibility for actions among group members. Review page 632 in your textbook.
   b.   For more information, see page 632 in your textbook.
   c.   This answer is incorrect because false consensus involves assuming that others agree with our positions much more than is real. Review page 632 in your textbook.
   d.   This answer is incorrect because impression management involves creating an impression that others have about us, which may or may not be true. Review page 632 in your textbook.

16.9   Cognitive dissonance is produced when we
   a.   This answer is incorrect because this situation would involve the traditional process of attitude change. Review page 633 in your textbook.
   b.   For more information, see page 633 in your textbook.
   c.   This answer is incorrect because this situation would involve a heuristic in decision making. Review page 633 in your textbook.
   d.   This answer is incorrect because this situation is not directly related to cognitive dissonance. Review page 633 in your textbook.

16.10   The idea that prejudice stems from economic competition among social groups is a central proposal of
   a.   This answer is incorrect because this theory involves making risky decisions. Review page 636 in your textbook.
   b.   This answer is incorrect because this theory involves a "us versus them" approach to prejudice. Review page 636 in your textbook.
   c.   This answer is incorrect because this theory involves learning prejudice through observation of others. Review page 636 in your textbook.
   d.   For more information, see page 636 in your textbook.

16.11 A _____ is a cognitive framework that suggests that all members of a specific social group have the same characteristics.
   a. This answer is incorrect because a Gestalt involves wholes, not necessarily the same characteristics. Review page 638 in your textbook.
   b. This answer is incorrect because contagion involves the spreading of an effect to other individuals. Review page 638 in your textbook.
   c. For more information, see page 638 in your textbook.
   d. This answer is incorrect because discrimination involves the prejudicial behavior. Review page 638 in your textbook.

16.12 Lisa has engaged in _____ when, to be accepted into the group, she wears a skirt to class, rather than the jeans she usually wears.
   a. This answer is incorrect because contagion involves the spreading of an effect to others. Review page 641 in your textbook.
   b. This answer is incorrect because obedience involves obeying a direct order. Review page 641 in your textbook.
   c. This answer is incorrect because compliance involves agreeing to a request. Review page 641 in your textbook.
   d. For more information, see page 641 in your textbook.

16.13 The foot-in-the-door technique is effective because of the pressure on individuals to
   a. For more information, see page 645 in your textbook.
   b. This answer is incorrect because rationality is not directly related to this technique. Review page 645 in your textbook.
   c. This answer is incorrect because competence is not directly related to this technique. Review page 645 in your textbook.
   d. This answer is incorrect because emotionality is not directly related to this technique. Review page 645 in your textbook.

16.14 A compliance tactic in which individuals try to create the image that they are very popular or very much in demand is called
   a. This answer is incorrect because ingratiation involves using tactics to get others to like us. Review page 645 in your textbook.
   b. This answer is incorrect because reciprocity involves treating others as we would like to be treated. Review page 645 in your textbook.
   c. For more information, see page 645 in your textbook.
   d. This answer is incorrect because this tactic is a part of reciprocity. Review page 645 in your textbook.

16.15 This type of love emphasizes feelings of strong attraction and sexual desire toward another person.
   a. This answer is incorrect because such love does not involve the strong attraction. Review page 650 in your textbook.
   b. This answer is incorrect because such love involves deep commitment and concern. Review page 650 in your textbook.
   c. For more information, see page 650 in your textbook.
   d. This answer is incorrect because such love involves commitment and concern for well-being. Review page 650 in your textbook.

16.16   The branch of psychology that investigates all aspects of social thought and social behavior is
    a.   This answer is incorrect because cognitive psychology does not deal with social aspects of behavior. Review page 619 in your textbook.
    b.   For more information, see page 619 in your textbook.
    c.   This answer is incorrect because attribution psychology deals only with attribution processes. Review page 619 in your textbook.
    d.   This answer is incorrect because dissonance psychology deals with attitude change. Review page 619 in your textbook.

16.17   You don't put much faith in the movie reviews in the paper, but when everyone you talk to agrees that the picture is terrific you decide to see it. The factor that convinced you is
    a.   This answer is incorrect because compliance is a social influence tactic. Review page 619 in your textbook.
    b.   This answer is incorrect because consistency involves how regularly a behavior occurs. Review page 619 in your textbook.
    c.   This answer is incorrect because distinctiveness involves how much a behavior stands out. Review page 619 in your textbook.
    d.   For more information, see page 619 in your textbook.

16.18   The correspondence bias is the tendency to explain the behavior of others in terms of _____ causes.
    a.   For more information, see page 620 in your textbook.
    b.   This answer is incorrect because the explanation is not in external terms. Review page 620 in your textbook.
    c.   This answer is incorrect because the explanation is not in stable terms. Review page 620 in your textbook.
    d.   This answer is incorrect because the explanation is not in unstable terms. Review page 620 in your textbook.

16.19   When we wish to make a decision quickly based on information that is already available using minimum effort, we will generally use
    a.   For more information, see page 624 in your textbook.
    b.   This answer is incorrect because dissonance is an attitude change concept. Review page 624 in your textbook.
    c.   This answer is incorrect because consensus is an attributional characteristic. Review page 624 in your textbook.
    d.   This answer is incorrect because recategorization is related to prejudice not decision making. Review page 624 in your textbook.

16.20   The process of _____ involves one or more individuals attempting to alter the attitudes of one or more other individuals.
    a.   This answer is incorrect because therapy is not designed to alter just attitudes. Review page 628 in your textbook.
    b.   This answer is incorrect because contagion involves the increase in emotion based upon social interaction. Review page 628 in your textbook.
    c.   For more information, see page 628 in your textbook.
    d.   This answer is incorrect because development is not relevant. Review page 628 in your textbook.

16.21   According to the elaboration likelihood model, little cognitive activity is performed and attitude change involves a seemingly automatic response to persuasion cues through the
   a. This answer is incorrect because there is no such route as the transient route. Review page 630 in your textbook.
   b. This answer is incorrect because there is no such route as the diffusion route. Review page 630 in your textbook.
   c. This answer is incorrect because the central route involves cognitive restructuring. Review page 630 in your textbook.
   d. For more information, see page 630 in your textbook.

16.22   According to cognitive dissonance theory, which of the following conditions is most likely to produce the greatest attitude change when asked to say something we do not believe to be true?
   a. This answer is incorrect because a large reward will not have that much impact on the attitude change. Review page 633 in your textbook.
   b. This answer is incorrect because a medium reward would have to be evaluated in terms of medium to what. Review page 633 in your textbook.
   c. For more information, see page 633 in your textbook.
   d. This answer is incorrect because no reward will have no impact according to dissonance theory. Review page 633 in your textbook.

16.23   Pressures toward thinking or acting like most other persons refers to
   a. This answer is incorrect because obedience is a change in behavior as a result of a command. Review page 641 in your textbook.
   b. This answer is incorrect because deindividualization involves the lack of personal identity of individuals in crowds. Review page 641 in your textbook.
   c. This answer is incorrect because prosocial behavior involves helping other individuals. Review page 641 in your textbook.
   d. For more information, see page 641 in your textbook.

16.24   A form of social influence in which individuals attempt to influence others through direct requests is called
   a. This answer is incorrect because conformity attempts to influence through peer pressure. Review page 644 in your textbook.
   b. For more information, see page 644 in your textbook.
   c. This answer is incorrect because obedience attempts to change behavior through commands. Review page 644 in your textbook.
   d. This answer is incorrect because consensus is not an social influence form. Review page 644 in your textbook..

16.25   Which of the following is not a factor related to troubled marital relationships?
   a. This answer is incorrect because jealousy is a factor related to marital relationships. Review page 652 in your textbook.
   b. This answer is incorrect because boredom is a factor related to marital relationships. Review page 652 in your textbook.
   c. This answer is incorrect because dissimilarities is a factor related to marital relationships. Review page 652 in your textbook.
   d. For more information, see page 652 in your textbook.

Chapter 16 - Practice Test Answers

Question	Answer
16.1	c
16.2	d
16.3	b
16.4	c
16.5	b
16.6	d
16.7	a
16.8	b
16.9	b
16.10	d
16.11	c
16.12	d
16.13	a
16.14	c
16.15	c
16.16	b
16.17	d
16.18	a
16.19	a
16.20	c
16.21	d
16.22	c
16.23	d
16.24	b
16.25	d